In Memory of Rochelle Nieman

Endings & Beginnings

Copyright © 2023 Charles Nieman

All rights reserved. No part of this book may be reproduced or used in any form without the prior written permission of the copyright owner.

To request permission, contact the publisher at publisher@charlesnieman.com.

Paperback: 979-8-9873761-0-2
Digital Online: 979-8-9873761-1-9
Ebook: 979-8-9873761-2-6

First edition February 2023.

Book Design by Aidan James Agency
Printed by El Paso Mail and Print Service

CSJ Ministries, Inc.
1000 Valley Crest Dr
El Paso, TX 79907

CharlesNieman.com

Manufactured in the United States of America

Endings & Beginnings

INDEX

Chapter One	P.12
Chapter Two	P.38
Chapter Three	P.60
Chapter Four	P.80
Chapter Five	P.100
Chapter Six	P.122

ENDINGS AND BEGINNINGS

WHEN LIFE DOESN'T PLAY ALONG

I CHOOSE TO BE RECOVERED

NO FRUIT LEFT IN THE FIELDS

YOU'VE GOT TO COMMIT TO THE MOUNTAIN

ENOUGH IS ENOUGH

YOUR LIGHT IS COMING

This book was ten years in the making. It is my story of how the Lord walked me through the trauma of the single greatest loss of my life, the death of my wife, Rochelle.

Why wait ten years? In fact, I have started and stopped this book several times. The reality is, I was not ready to be as open as I felt I needed to be in order to reveal many personal things I experienced, and overcame.

It is my hope and prayer, that what I learned from the Lord will help you or someone you know and love to experience healing and restoration!

The truths I share with you have become a part of my daily life. They do not live somewhere in my past. They live in me everyday, and they continue to take my life forward. They will do the same for you or someone you care about.

Thank you for being willing to hear my story and for sharing in my victory!

Charles Nieman

We all know that there are times in our lives when life doesn't play along, and it should not catch us by surprise, because in John the 16th chapter, verse 33, Jesus said, in this world you will have temptations, tests and trials. You will have them but be of good cheer. The King James text says a more accurate translation is, "take courage for I have overcome the world."

In Mark the 4th chapter, Jesus reveals to us that when the Word of God comes into your life, satan will bring persecution and affliction against you to try to drive you away from the very Word that God is bringing into your life, to ignite your life and to give you the God-kind of life. The goal is to try to cause you to become offended, to give up, because of pressure, circumstances, people coming against you, and acts of hatred. The question is not "if" these temptations, tests and trials will happen to us. The question is how we respond to them. Will we collapse under the pressure, or will we break through?

CHAPTER ONE

This doesn't happen all your life – day after day, every week, month, year. In Psalm 23: 1-6, half of one verse talks about a not-so-good day, "Yea, though I walk through the valley of the shadow of death..." But the other five and a half verses are spectacular. "The Lord is my shepherd. I shall not want. He leads me beside the still waters. He takes me into green pastures. He restores my soul. He sets a table before me in the presence of my enemies. Surely goodness and mercy will follow me. I'll dwell in the house of the Lord forever. And even when I'm in the valley of the shadow of death, I will fear no evil for your rod and your staff, they will comfort me."

Psalm 23: 1-6 has always strengthened me when thinking about my life and keeping perspective. In all of that, we see that God is present. God is there. God is real. God is here for us.

Now, if you will allow me, in this book, I am going to share with you from my heart to your heart. This is what I have done since my wife of 42 years, Rochelle, passed away. I'm not saying that what I've learned is the only way to respond when life doesn't play along, but what I found worked and is working, and there is no reason why it can't work in your life because God is not a respecter of persons (Acts 10:38).

Let me give you a little history. On May the 4th of 2012, Rochelle was diagnosed with stage 4 ovarian cancer. That began an almost nine-month journey for her, for me, my children, our church family, our extended family, and our friends, culminating with her passing away on 8:45 in the morning of December the 30th, 2012.

When Rochelle passed away that morning, I was at church. I did the 8:30 a.m. service, the first of our three Sunday services. The reason why I was at church was because she told me on Saturday night that I was going to church on Sunday morning and doing the services.

I learned, after 42 years of marriage, there were certain things just not worth arguing with Rochelle about, and I could tell by the look in her eye that this was one of them. So, I did the Saturday night service and went home. She asked me how it was. I told her about it. She was so happy. But I had already decided that I wasn't going to go the next day and I guess she sensed it.

She said, "Now, you are going to do the services tomorrow."

I said, "No, I think I'm going to stay with you."

She said, "No. You are going to do the services tomorrow. You've been missing a lot of church. The church needs to see you. You need to be there. You're their pastor. You need to go to church."

So, I went. I did the first service. When the service was over, my security team came and got me, and I knew when they did — I knew when they came to get me that she was gone.

CHAPTER ONE

"Father, I can't screw this up. Help me."

I made the decision that I would leave and go home to be with my family, and I would run the recording of the 8:30 a.m. service in the 10:30 a.m. and 12:30 p.m. services, and our praise and worship team, who knew everything, stepped up and went forward, all our staff did. No one could say anything about her passing because we needed time to process what had happened and decide how we would release the news.

That afternoon, we announced her death through social media, which we thought was the best way to do it, and things began to move forward from there.

That morning, when I left the church and was driving home after the 8:30 service, the 10:30 service was starting. I had to stay awhile and take care of some things before I left.

I found myself in my car driving home unable to call anyone. I couldn't call any of my friends. "Why, pastor?" Because all my friends are pastors. They were all in church. Around the world, they were in church. Even the ones on the other part of the world were in their evening services or already asleep. So, I found myself with a 20- to 25-minute car ride by myself, knowing that when I got home, my family would be there, and my life was going into a realm I had never experienced. I had to make good choices...my family needed me. My church. My staff. My friends. People I didn't know yet were going to be affected by how I responded.

This was me. I'm not saying everyone responds this way. This is my story.

As I was driving in my car, I had some Christian music on. I was in shock to be honest with you. The last thing Rochelle said to me on Saturday night was, "I'm going to get better." And so I never allowed my mind to go anywhere but there. I always kept my mind there! Does that make sense to you? I never allowed my mind to go anywhere other than she was going to get better, and that's the way it should be.

I was driving home, and I prayed this prayer, and I quote. I said, "Father, I can't screw this up. Help me."

What I meant by "I can't screw this up" is that I can't make the wrong move. I've got to go in the right direction. I have to make good choices. I have to make good decisions. I can't screw this up. Now, "this" is a huge word. "This" means my personal life. "This" means my kids. "This" means my grandkids. "This" means Rochelle's legacy, my legacy, whatever that may be, and the magnificent, gigantic church that is affecting the lives of so many thousands of people every year. I said, "I can't screw this up."

CHAPTER ONE

Now, you may not talk that way. That's the way I talk. I also prayed, "Lord, help me."

Now, the first thing I knew I had to do, if you are taking notes, you might write this down: The first thing I knew I had to do — no one had to say anything to me. I didn't have to have a burning bush. I knew this in my heart because it is something that I have practiced for years in my life, but because of the circumstance, it took on a new, heightened meaning in my life. The first thing I knew I had to do when life doesn't play along. Pray. This would be the first thing I would tell you to do. I would tell you to pray and ask God to help you not screw up, and, number two, I knew in my heart that as soon as physically possible, I had to get in church. I had to get in a church service as soon as physically possible. I had to do it. Let me show you why.

Isaiah **40:31**. I knew this had to be my response and it had to be my <u>continual response</u>. I could not do anything other than what I knew would work and would produce what I needed and what you may need in your life. There is no telling what you are in or have gone through that could be defined as life not playing along. It is a reality of life. Sometimes things don't work the way you planned. They didn't work the way you thought. Relationships, businesses, health issues, different things in your life, not what you planned. Not what you planned, but yet there it is. And now what are you going to do? What are you going to do?

I'm not being critical when I say this, because I understand how things happen. What are you going to do? A lot of people crawl into a corner, emotionally, physically, mentally, spiritually. But I knew in my heart I could not do that, and if I did that, Rochelle may come down and slap me in the back of the head. I wouldn't mind seeing her again, but I don't want her to come and be upset with me!

I knew I had to move in the right direction, and the first thing I knew, driving in my car that day, was I've got to get in church. And the reason why I said that is because of this verse, Isaiah 40:31: "But they that wait upon the Lord."

"But they that wait upon the Lord…"

A doctrine has been built around that not-so-good translation. We get the idea that we are just waiting.

"What are you doing?"

"I'm waiting on the Lord. Pray for me. I'm waiting on the Lord. Just waiting on the Lord."

It's really a poor translation. It's not a poor translation based on how the word "wait" was used back when the King James Bible was translated; but, in our world today, the word "waiting" has taken on the idea that we have to learn to wait. In the literal Hebrew text, the phrase "they that wait upon Lord," means "they that gather together before the Lord."

In Matthew 16, Jesus said: "Upon this rock, I will build my church." The word "church", in the Greek text, means "my gathering." The church can be called Jesus' gathering.

CHAPTER ONE

In Matthew 18, Jesus said, "If two or more gather together in my name." He's not talking about two people meeting in a coffee shop and both being Christians. No. He is talking about church. He is talking about when the church comes together, when the body of Christ gathers before the Lord. When we come together in services, He said, "There will I be in the midst of them." Right?

Isaiah 40:31, "They that gather together." When life is not playing along, the first thing you've got to do is get in church as much as you possibly can. Don't listen to the devil tell you to stay away from the house of God. Don't let the devil push you away from God. Don't let the devil separate you from the house of God. Get in the house of God!

I know what you're thinking because I used to think it too. "Charles, that doesn't make sense. It doesn't make sense that I'm hurting and got a bad deal, or I've got something going on in my life, and if I come to church, people don't even know I'm hurting." No, they don't. But He does and He is here in the midst of us.

I can't tell you why He set it up this way. All I can tell you is He set it up this way. So be smart enough to go in the direction of the very thing that you need. Because look at what He says. "They that gather together before the Lord shall renew their strength."

Remember, earlier I said I was going to talk from my heart, right? When I was driving in that car, "I thought where am I going to get the strength?" I'm telling you, physically, I was exhausted. My kids were exhausted. Mentally, I was exhausted. Spiritually, I felt like I was running on fumes. Rochelle's passing away didn't relieve any of that. It upped it. Do you understand what I mean by that? It didn't get better. It upped it. The exhaustion didn't leave.

I'm going to be honest with you, I am so glad that over the years, I have memorized scripture, and they live in me. They live in me. (Hebrews 4:16). I didn't have to run to a concordance. I didn't have to Google "strength" in the Bible. This verse popped into my mind, when I thought, "I have got to have strength!" And the first thing I thought was, "I've got to get in church," because when you gather together with God's people before the Lord, He will renew your strength.

I don't know how He does it. I don't understand how He does it. I don't know why He doesn't just zap you in your backyard, but that's not the way He set it up. He said He's going to renew your strength when you gather together.

Not only that, look at what else He said. "You shall renew your strength. You will mount up with wings as of eagles."

That is what I needed to hear. I needed to get some wind under my wings. Am I making sense to you? I needed some wind under my wings, and it's here. It is here when you gather together. The more you are in the house of God, the more you are in the gatherings of Christ, the more your strength is going to be renewed, the more wind is going to get under your wings. And as a result, what is going to happen to you? Look at it, Isaiah 40:31 states, "you will run and not be weary. You will walk and not faint." The word "faint" means you won't throw in the towel, you won't quit, you won't lay down.

When Rochelle died, it just so happened that we were having New Year's Eve service the next night. People began to call me from all over the world when they heard about Rochelle. People called me, and asked, "Charles, what are you going to do?" And I said, "Well, I'm going to go to church tomorrow night."

One person said to me, "You're doing what?"

I said, "We have New Year's Eve service tomorrow night and I'm going."

They asked, "But you're not speaking, are you?"

I said, "Absolutely, I'm speaking."

Some suggested I should stay home. I said, "No, you see, Isaiah 40:31 says if I gather together, God will renew my strength."

I'm telling you, you can ask my children, my friends. All day New Year's Eve, all I kept saying was, "I can't wait for church to get here."

Church started at 7:00 p.m. Do you know where I was at 5:00 p.m.? I was waiting in the back of the church building. I left my house at **4:30** p.m. I said, "I'm tired of sitting here. I'm getting to the house of God. I'm going to go there because the closer I get to that service, the quicker I am getting my strength renewed." Does that make sense to you?

Later that week, I did the Wednesday night service. For lack of a better term, I MC'd Rochelle's memorial service that Friday night. I did the Saturday night service. I did all the Sunday morning services. I took extra speaking engagements. I went to services that I was not even speaking at. Why? Because I'm a preacher? No. Because I want my strength renewed. I want wind to be beneath my wings.

I am in every praise and worship service. I don't sit in the back. I don't sit out. I don't miss the praise and worship services. Why? Because God inhabits the praises of His people, Psalm 22:6. And Psalm 8 says, "he ordained praise to still the enemy and quiet the avenger." So, I get in every praise and worship service. I'm down front. I've got my hands up. I'm singing those songs. I'm letting God do His God thing in my life. Doesn't this make sense to you?

Honestly, a mistake a lot of people make when life doesn't play along is they start skipping church. They stay away from church. The devil tells them, "Don't go down there. They don't understand. They don't know." The reality is a lot of the people don't know and they don't understand what you're going through. The reality is that even the ones who do understand and do know what you're going through can't renew your strength. And I don't mean that in a bad way. Listen to me. I am being honest with you, my friends couldn't renew my strength. They all loved me. They all prayed for me. They reached out to me. They called me. They sent me texts. They checked on me all the time. And I'm very grateful for all of that. It means the world to me. But none of them have that ability, and I don't look to them for that. I don't look to my kids to renew my strength. The only one who can renew my strength is He that is in our midst.

So don't separate yourself! Don't run _from_, run _to_ where God has promised He would renew your strength and give you power and endurance so that you can run when you need to run and walk when you need to walk. Either way, you'll be able to do life. Stay in His House. Stay connected to His Body. His strength will renew you.

A few days later, I was praying, and the Lord encouraged me to re-read John 11.

John 11:1. This is the story of Lazarus, and Mary and Martha, his sisters. And the word came to Jesus that said he was sick. Verse 3, "Lord, behold, he whom you love is sick." This is a family that Jesus knew personally. He cared for them. They were close to him. They weren't casual acquaintances. Martha said, "He whom you love is sick." So, He was close to them and probably spent time at their house.

It was Martha who had washed Jesus' feet with her tears and wiped His feet with her hair. That is how close the connection was.

Word comes that Lazarus died. We pick up in verse 18: "Now, Bethany was nigh unto Jerusalem, about 15 furlongs away. And many of the Jews came to Martha and Mary, to comfort them concerning their brother."

That's nice, don't you agree? It's nice.

"Then Martha, as soon as she heard that Jesus was coming, went and met him; but, Mary sat still in the house."

"Then said Martha unto Jesus, Lord, if you had been here, my brother had not died."

Wow, what a statement? That is quite a statement, don't you agree? I mean, that is quite a statement of faith, of believing!

"But I know that even now," Martha said, "whatsoever you will ask of God, God will give it to you."

Martha said something without saying it. Did you catch on to what she said? She lays down a heavy insinuation: "If you would have been here, he wouldn't have died." But even now -- I mean, I'm not telling you what to do, but *even now, whatever you ask, it can happen.* Watch how Jesus responds to her.

Jesus said unto her, "Your brother shall rise again."

Whoa! Now, watch how she responds. Martha said unto Him, "I know that he shall rise again..." Right there, there should have been a period, but here's a great truth and a great revelation, "...in the resurrection at the last day."

What I learned in this story has meant so much to me. What I learned in this story is — be careful that you don't respond like Martha did. Martha said, "If you had been here, he would have been great; and someday, he will be great again."

When life isn't playing along, what is really hard is being in the <u>now</u>, because now is where all the pain is. If you can go far enough back in the past, there is no pain. If you can go far enough into the future, there won't be any pain. But, we can't live in the past or in the future; we only live in the NOW. She said, "If you had been" and "I know someday." Do you see what she did? She went past, she went future.

Now, watch what Jesus does. Look at the next verse. She's talking past. She's talking future. Jesus says unto her, "I Am." Present tense!

You and I have lived in our New Testament world so long that we are used to reading the gospels, and we're used to Jesus saying, "I am the bread of life," "I am the vine," I am this, I am that. We are used to it. If you were there that day -- the people of that day did not use that phrase. They did not talk that way.

If you understand this, then you will understand why, when Jesus said, "I am the bread of life," why the religious leaders said he should be stoned. It was not because He said He was the bread of life. They didn't even get that. It was because He used the term "I Am," in reference to Himself. The reason they were so upset was because there is only one other place in the Bible where that phrase appears. It is Exodus 3:14. Moses is talking to the burning bush, and Moses says to the bush, "Who do I say sent me?" In the King James text, it says you tell them, "I Am that I Am sent you." But, we know that the phrase "I Am" is also the Hebrew name "Yahweh." It was the first time in the Bible that God gave them His own name.

But now, God is asked, for the first time, "Who do I say sent me? What's your name?"

He said, "You tell them Yahweh sent you."

Yahweh is an Old Testament name that means "Redeemer, Deliverer, Savior." The part of the Godhead that was in that burning bush that day talking to Moses was none other than Jesus Christ before He took upon Himself flesh.

Why? Why was He there? Why was Jesus talking to Moses? Because Moses was going to deliver the people out of the bondage of Egypt. The part of the Godhead that we also know as The Trinity, Jesus, came to Moses as the redeemer, the deliverer and the savior, and He said, "You tell them Yahweh sent you."

Do you know that the name "Yahweh" in the Hebrew also means "the Hand of Grace Pierced by Grace". So, He said, "You tell them the Hand of Grace Pierced by Grace has sent you."

CHAPTER ONE

Standing there in front of Martha, Jesus said to her, "I Am." He was saying, "I Am, Yahweh, the Redeemer, the Deliverer, the Savior.

"The Redeemer, the Deliverer, the Savior, the God that was in the burning bush is standing in front of you right now. The same God that delivered Israel is standing in front of you right now. That same God is here right now."

He didn't say, "I Am the great I was." He didn't say, "I'm the great going to be." He was saying, "No, no. We are not living in the past. We're not living in the future."

Here is the thing the Lord revealed to me. I couldn't live in the past. I couldn't think about the future. I had to let Him in. "Who, Charles?" <u>The now God</u>. I had to let the now God into my now life. I had to let Him in where all the pain was. I had to let Him into my now. I couldn't think about what was. I couldn't think about what would be. I had to let Him into this moment in my life!

That is the mistake a lot of people make. They want to do it themselves. They want to sort it out themselves. They want to handle it themselves. They want to have that room called "pain" and go into it by themselves and then come out and find the Lord, when, in fact, the Lord wants to go in that room with you. He is the only one, the only one, that has the ability to go in that room with you and deal with it, and He knows how to deal with it!

And here is how He deals with it. Are you ready? He said, "I am the resurrection. I am the resurrection. I am the resurrection."

Get ready!

"Resurrection," in the Greek text, means "I am the stand up and the recovery. I am the stand up and the recovery. I am the stand up and the recovery. I am the stand up and the recovery. I am the stand up and the recovery. I am the stand up and the recovery."

I'm not saying this for you. I'm saying it for me! I like to hear it.

"I am the stand up and the recovery. I am the stand up" – I just love all of the imagery unfolding in my mind – "I am the stand up and the recovery."

Now, you say it – THE I AM IS MY STAND UP AND MY RECOVERY!! Say it again!!

One night, I was lying in my bed, and I had been crying for a long time, and I got up. Jesus brought me back to this chapter, and I looked at it. He said this into my heart and He's going to say it into your heart right now. He said, "I am the stand up and the recovery. You are down. You can't get up. Let me stand up, and I'll stand you up with Me when I stand up on the inside of you."

He said, "You don't have to stand up. I am -- I am the stand up. You don't have to get up." You see, I had been questioning, "God, how am I going to get up from this?"

CHAPTER ONE

He said, "You're not. You can't." He said to me, "This is way beyond your ability, Charles. But that's okay, We're here with you. I am the stand up."

I saw this image on the inside of me. I could see this as clearly now as when I saw it in 2013. I saw Him, in me, down with me. Him in me, down with me. And He stood up, and because He's in me, when He stood up, I got up with Him. "I am in the stand up and the recovery."

"I am in the stand up and the recovery!" He is my stand up! He is your stand up! You can get up from the floor. No matter how hard you fell, no matter how hard you are hit, no matter how long you have been down, no matter how many times you've tried to get up and couldn't – **HE IS YOUR STAND UP!** He will get you up.

He said, "I am the resurrection and the life."

The next part of the verse took me several months to get. I got the first part. I got "stand up" really quick. I am still seeing what "recovery" means to Him. I do not define recovery. He defines recovery. I am not defining recovery. I don't know what recovery means to me over the rest of my life. I have seen some of it already. Without us doing anything different or increasing our budget or advertising or anything new, January through March of 2013, our church grew 30 percent. I would say God said, "I got you here. I am going to give you some recovery here. This is to let you know I am still working."

I have had doors and opportunities open to me. Some really cool things have happened in my personal life, all of which is really nice, but I'm letting Him define my recovery.

Jesus said, "I am the resurrection and the life." Now, I want you to listen to what I'm going to tell you. If you don't hear me what I'm going to say, you are going to misunderstand me and you're going to walk away from reading this book and you're not going to think good of me.

Jesus said, "I am the stand up and the recovery and the life." In the Greek and English New Testament dictionary, the word "life" in this verse means, "I am the life that satisfies because I dwell in your life." Let me say it again: I am the life that satisfies because I dwell in your life.

Now, listen carefully. When the Lord brought me to this verse, I saw that He is my stand up and my recovery. I focused on that reality and my life began to go forward. That truth really helped me, it strengthened me. As I said, my life began to go forward. I started confessing that Jesus is my Stand Up and my Recovery several times a day. I put my heart and my soul into believing Jesus, the I Am, was standing me up and bringing me recovery to my life, my family, and our church. Then some time later, He brought me back to this verse. Why? Because in the beginning, I wasn't ready for the second part of the promise. As I recovered, I had to take the next step. Jesus said, "I am the life that satisfies because I dwell in your life."

CHAPTER ONE

When He revealed this truth to me, He was very gentle with me. He knew I was going to struggle emotionally with what I needed to accept. You may also struggle, that's ok. It is a part of recovery.

I loved Rochelle with all my heart. There was no part of my heart that she didn't have. I missed her terribly; but, I had to decide and accept that He is the life that satisfies. I loved Rochelle with all my heart, but she didn't give me life. I didn't give her life. He gave us life!

One morning, I said out loud, "At 8:45 in the morning on December 30th, Rochelle left me. Jesus stayed."

She didn't want to leave. If there was anybody in the history of world that got to heaven and Peter had to come out and talk to her about coming in, it was Rochelle, I promise you. There is a very good chance that she stood out there in her high heels saying, "I'm not going in. No, I am not supposed to be here. Somebody needs to take me back." Wouldn't surprise me at all. And her big old purse. Little girl, gigantic purses.

Do you understand what I'm saying to you? What He is saying to you? It is vital to your stand up and recovery that you understand what it means to you that Jesus is the life that satisfies dwelling in your life.

If you don't understand this and you don't embrace this, then thoughts will come into your mind like, "I have no reason to live. I have no reason to go on. I have no reason..." That is all understandable, but it is not accurate. You do have a reason to go on, because He is the life that satisfies!

Do not put that burden on someone who can't carry it. Do not put the responsibility, to be your life that satisfies, on a child or a parent or a friend or a spouse. They can't carry it! Only "I Am" can be that in your life. I can live, I can go forward, I can be satisfied, even though my loved one is gone, because Jesus did not go. He did not leave me or you. He is our life that satisfies, dwelling in our lives.

Let's look at verse 33 and 38. What you are going to see now will really strengthen you and may change your life perspective. It did mine.

Verse 33: "When Jesus therefore saw her weeping, and the Jews also weeping which came with her, He groaned in his spirit, and was troubled."

Verse 38: "Jesus therefore again groaning in Himself came to the grave."

"Groaning" is a very powerful word. What it literally means is, "He became indignant." It also means, He "got his roar back." Think about this. Jesus became indignant. He began to roar in his spirit. The word "indignant" means "to become angry at an injustice."

You may need to get your roar back! You may need to get up out of the corner. You may need to quit holding on and crying. You may need to quit telling yourself that your life is over. You need to get indignant. You may need to get some "Grrr" back in your heart. I sure needed to. I had to get back into life, back into the race, back into the fight. It is alright to get angry at the unjust loss in your life. Jesus did! He got angry at the loss of His friend. He got angry at the pain He was seeing around Him. This is vital to your recovery! You need to get up and go take life back and go live the life that God wants you to live and do it with a sense of indignation in your life and a roar in your heart!

Jesus gave you and me these scriptures. Get angry at the injustice. What happened to Rochelle, to our family, to our church was not right! I am not asking God to teach me how to cope with it. I am not here to cope with it. I don't like it. I am still mad about it. I am going to live my life with a vengeance because of it. I've got my roar back. I am angry at the injustice of it all!

I want to show you another great truth that brought recovery to my life. Again, I ask you to open your heart to what I am going to share with you. This truth may surprise you, but it will also heal you and take your life forward.

II Corinthians 11:23-28: In this great chapter, the Apostle Paul lists all of the things that were done to him while he was preaching the gospel. I will summarize. He was beaten with rods, he was stoned, he was shipwrecked, he was lied to, he was deceived, he was stolen from by friends, by non-friends. He was in danger for his life by countrymen, by believers and by false brethren, or people who acted like believers, but were not. He was shipwrecked and lost everything. He was beaten five times with whips. He was beaten three times with rods. Can you imagine being hit with rods three times, until you pass out? He was left in the ocean a day and a night. He went through times of forced fasting because of lack of food. He didn't have enough water at times, he suffered from the cold because of a lack of clothes.

It is unbelievable what he went through! As I read these verses, I noticed something that hit me like a brick! What I saw as I read and re-read what Paul went through is that he never said, "Why me?"

He could have. If there is anyone who has ever lived, who had a right to stand before God and say, "Why me?" It is Paul. I imagine he could have said, "Peter should be going through this. He is the one that denied you. Remember, Lord? Three times, he denied you. Peter, the one you gave the keys to the kingdom, the same Peter who was going to build the church. He denied you three times!

"I've never denied you. Peter is living in Jerusalem, as happy as he can be. Now you are sending him to Rome. Just great, good for Peter. I am out here getting my brains beat out. Why me?" Not one time did Paul say, "Why me?"

What I discovered in this chapter, led me to say to myself: If Paul never said, "Why me?" Charles is never going to say, "Why me?" I don't have any right to say, "Why me?" I want to tell you what this did for me. It gave me the right perspective about what happened to me. Here is what I mean by perspective.

"Get up, don't feel sorry for yourself, don't allow this to become an excuse to give up."

I'm going to say this, and I don't want you to get mad at me when I say it. When I read that chapter and realized Paul never said, "Why me?" This is what I said. "God, I am not the first man that lost his wife and I won't be the last. The whole universe did not align itself and come after me." I got my perspective.

Was what happened lousy? You're darn right, it was lousy! But, I wasn't the first and I won't be the last.

It helped me to quit feeling sorry for myself. I could have, I had "the right" to throw myself a massive pity party and I did for a while, but what good is that going to produce? Is feeling sorry for myself going to strengthen me, get me up off the floor, bring recovery to my life and my family? **NO**. In fact, asking "Why me?" is going to hold me down, it is going to keep me in the past, it is going to rob me of the life Jesus came to give me, and over time, will probably pull me into depression.

Asking, "Why me?" could also lead me into being upset with God. It can cause me to begin thinking that God didn't do right by me, which can cause me to become displeased with God, which leads to resentment and finally to bitterness. There was nothing in that picture that I wanted.

I said to myself, "Charles, don't go to that place of asking, "why me?" You are not the first person who felt life didn't go the way you thought, and you won't be the last! Get up, don't feel sorry for yourself, don't become a martyr, don't allow this to become an excuse to give up. Paul didn't, and I'm not either!"

Let's review for a moment, John 16:33, Jesus said, "In the world, you will have temptations, tests and trials, but have good courage, for I have overcome the world." Hard times, tests, trials, things not going as we thought or planned, are a part of life. Lousy things happen to all of us.

In Mark the 4th chapter, verses 14-20, Jesus revealed to us that when the Word of God comes into our lives, one of the reactions that can happen in our lives is that temptations, tests and trials can come against our lives to try to separate us from the impact of the Word of God.

In this book, I am sharing what the Lord has shown me to do when life gets bad. I am not saying this is the only way to handle these times. It is what He showed me to do, and it has worked for me. It is what I have done and continue to do since all of this happened with my amazing wife Rochelle.

I am sharing with you the path the Lord led me down as revealed to me in and through His Word.

CHAPTER TWO

These truths have brought incredible power, comfort and strength to my life and have enabled me to go forward and keep going forward and not collapse. Don't think I didn't think about quitting. I did think about it. But, as my Pastor Tommy Barnett has said to me, "There is nothing wrong with thinking about quitting, just don't quit. I didn't really think about quitting seriously. Someone said to me once, "I bet, the morning Rochelle died, you thought about quitting."

No, I did not. Why? Because I'm not a quitter!

I am not saying that if someone does think about quitting that there is something wrong with them. I am just telling you the truth, I never seriously thought about quitting on God, on the church, on life.

That morning, when I was driving home from church, after finding out that Rochelle had passed away, I had some alone time in my car. As I said to you before, I could not call my friends, because all my friends are pastors, and as a result, they were all in church or in bed depending upon where they lived in the world.

So, I had about 20 to 25 minutes by myself in my car. I had on some worship music. As I was driving, I prayed this prayer. It is not a real formal prayer, not a real religious prayer, but it was my prayer. I prayed, "Father, I can't screw this up. Help me."

I believe that prayer brought about an amazing set of truths to my life. Looking back on it now, I see that at the moment I prayed that prayer, I was deciding, at that moment, I wasn't going to screw this up! In that crucial moment, I made a decision, a conscious decision, to go forward, to not collapse, to not wave a white flag of surrender, or to say, "How can I go on? I've lost my incredible wife."

I had a resolve in me, and I believe that resolve came, not because of me or my personality, but because of Christ who is in me (Colossians 1:27) to go forward. From that prayer, I see now that the Lord began to quickly set things in motion in my heart and show me the things I am sharing with you.

I want to emphasize to you again that the first thing I knew I had to go back in church. I needed to get among the people of God. I needed to get in the house of God. I needed to get in as many church services as I possibly could. I cannot emphasize this enough to you and for you. Isaiah 40:31, "They that gather before the Lord shall renew their strength." I knew that the more time I could get in the house of God, the more time I could spend in praise and worship and under the teaching of the Word and among God's people, the stronger I would get. In Matthew 18:20, Jesus said, "Where two or three gather together, I will be in the midst of them." The word "gather" refers to the church.

I needed to get in His presence. His presence is heaven to me. I needed to get where I knew He was. I know He is in me, but I needed His presence that comes in the gathering of His church. There are things God will do for you in church that you can't

get anywhere else in this universe or anywhere else on the earth. You can only get them at church.
You can read this and argue. You can say, "Well, I don't think that's right." Let me remind you of something. You didn't write the Bible. You are not God. You didn't create all this. You didn't invent all this. He set these principles in place, and you are going to benefit from them if you do it the way He set it up. The more I am in the house of God, the more I am in praise and worship, the more I am with His church, the stronger I get.

Before we look at some new truths, let's remember John 11:25 – Jesus is our stand and our recovery. Jesus is my stand up and my recovery. I didn't have to stand up. I just had to let Him stand up in me. If I did let Him stand up in me, then I will stand up because He is in me. And not only was He my stand up and my recovery, but He is also my life that satisfies because He dwells in my life!

Let's get into some new truth. Are you ready? I have some really, really powerful things to share with you. We are going to study from the life of David as recorded in I Samuel 30:1-**8**.

Before we study this incident in David's life, I want to give you some background so you understand the context. David, at this time, is running from Saul because Saul is trying to kill him. David has been anointed the new king and Saul wants to hold on to what he no longer has the right to hold on to. Therefore, he is trying to kill David. David and his men have fled to the land of the Philistines.

"Jesus is my stand up and my recovery."

While he is living there, the Philistines were going to war with the Nation of Israel. David tells his men, "Because we are here, under the protection of the king, we must go to war against our brethren with the Philistines because they are providing us with protection." They're living in a town called Ziklag. They leave their families in Ziklag and they go to meet the Philistine Army.

When they get there, the king of the Philistines says to David, I Samuel 29:6, "David, while you are living here, you are living upright." David was living the right way.

You can't say that about all of David's life. It is in the scripture, there were times in David's life when he did not live upright. But this was a time in his life when David was doing it right. He was living right. He was doing the right things.

The king said, "The princes of the Philistines don't trust you. They're not going to let you fight with us, so go back to Ziklag." It was a day and a half of travel to where the army was and a day and a half back.

CHAPTER TWO

We will pick up the story in chapter 30, verse 1: "It came to pass when David and his men were come to Ziklag on the third day, the Amalekites had invaded the south and Ziklag and smitten Ziklag and burned it with fire. And had taken the women captives that were therein; they slew not any, either great nor small, but carried them away and went on their way. David and his men came to the city, and behold it was burned with fire; and their wives and their sons and their daughters were taken captives. Then David and the people that were with him, lifted up their voice and wept, until they had no more power to weep."

What a horrible day. They lost their wives, their children, their possessions, and their houses were burned. All while David and his men were living right. Here we see one of the realities of life, whether we like it or not, sometimes really lousy things happen to good people. It has happened to me, it has happened to you. Sometimes real crummy things happen to good people.

While David was living right and doing the right thing, the Amalekites came, took all their possessions, burned their city, took their wives, their sons, and their daughters as captives. Can you imagine the fear, the panic, grief, the guilt they must have felt as they were riding up to the city and seeing the smoke at Ziklag? When they got to Ziklag, everything they held dear was gone. Everything they had built was gone. The things they cared about the most in life were gone. All they had was a city on fire and their grief, and the awareness they had done nothing to deserve it.

Notice the verse, "that they lifted up their voice and wept until they had no power to weep," David and the men with him wept until they had no more power to weep. I will be honest with you, when all of this happened to Rochelle, I wept a lot. Every time I have felt like weeping, I had the power to weep. There were more tears to be shed. But David and his men went to a place that I didn't know, and I didn't want to know, the place where there was no more power to weep. They were emotionally spent.

I can understand it. You may also understand that kind of grief. Reality is that at times, life does not play along, things go sideways, we lost a loved one, a relationship we thought we would enjoy all of our lives ends. The list goes on and on. The end result is grief enters our lives. The question is not whether grief will enter our lives, the question is can we rise above it, and if we can, how? God says, "Yes, you can rise above grief," and He shows us how through David's life. Let's keep reading.

Jump with me down to verse 6: "And David was greatly distressed, for the people spoke of stoning him."

Oh, my gosh. David's day now goes from bad to worse. Not only has he lost his family and his possessions, but he also watched the men he cares about, the men who were closest to him, lose their wives and children and possessions, and now they want to stone him. Can you imagine?

Most of us cannot truly fathom this kind of loss and devastation unless you have lived through a tornado or a hurricane or a huge fire. Not sure many of us really understand this kind of destruction. Remember, this was an entire community, 600 families. Everything was gone that they cared about. Then the men who David was grieving with turned against David and begin to talk about stoning him.

The Bible tells us why. Here is an important lesson you must watch out for when life doesn't play along. "For the people spoke of stoning him because of the soul of all the people was grieved." The literal Hebrew says, "their souls became bitter." They became bitter.

Let's look at bitterness for a moment. In scripture, there are two negative human emotions that are referred to as having a root. One is the love of money and the other is bitterness. Hate, lust, resentment, unforgiveness — as destructive as they are, none of them are spoken of as having a root. The love of money is not mentioned in the story of David, but bitterness is.

The dictionary defines bitterness as intense hostility. One of the destructive forces you must watch out for in your life when life doesn't play along, is that you don't become bitter. All the men who were around David, except David, became bitter. They became intensely hostile. That is why they picked up rocks to stone him. That is why they wanted to kill him. Their bitterness began to manifest itself in their intense hostility.

You know and I know the danger of roots. In El Paso, years ago somebody decided that we should plant non-bearing mulberry trees all over the city. They went up everywhere. They are great providers of shade; but, what we have discovered was that if you plant one in the backyard, it will send out its roots and those roots will grow under your house, come up in your front yard, buckle your front yard sidewalk, and grow into the sewer line in the middle of the street to get water.

That is the nature of those trees and their roots. The reality is that if you allow bitterness to get into your life, even if you can justify it, over time, you will not be able to control the bitterness. After five, 10, 15 years, you are going to discover bitterness has sent its roots out into almost every area of your life. Before you know it, you are going to be in your 60s and nobody will want to be around you, no one will want to come to your house, no one will want to talk to you. Do you know why? Because your bitterness, your intense hostility, is going to drive everyone away. Even though you never intended to become bitter in those other areas of your life, right?

Maybe you are bitter over something that happened when you were a child or you're bitter about your ex, or you're bitter about something that happened on a job or you're bitter about how your family treated you or didn't support you, the list of justified reasons to be bitter goes on and on.

David's men could justify their bitterness. I would never say these men had no reason to be bitter. If I had said that to them, I think they may have said back to me, "We've got a rock for you too, boy. All we've got left are rocks. Just wait in line, because once we get rid of hotshot King David over here, we are going to take care of you, stranger."

This is very powerful, and I'm spending some time on this because I have seen the impact of bitterness up close and personal. I've seen what bitterness can do. I know people today who are living by themselves, because of their bitterness and the intense hostility it produces, and they can justify it. Something happened to them that was terrible. Life didn't play along. It was wrong. Instead of dealing with it the way the Bible teaches us how to deal with it, they went down the road of bitterness.

That is what we should see with David and his men, right? Everybody had the same thing happen to them. David and his men came to a crossroads. The men with David went down one road, but David went down a different road. When I saw that, I said, "I can either end up like David's men or I could end up like David."

We don't name our children after the men that picked up rocks, but we do name our children after David. Even with all his faults, he was still a man after God's own heart. He still wrote more of the Bible than anybody. He wrote the book of Psalms. Incredible man. But he had to make a choice, and he made the right one!

I had to decide in my life which road I was going to take. I decided to take another path, the path David took, the path away from bitterness! I could have allowed bitterness into my soul. I could have even justified it. I decided that bitterness was not going to get in me, in any shape or form. I wasn't going to become bitter because I knew where it would go. You can't keep bitterness in one area. It has roots, it is going to spread and will eventually, infect other areas of your life. It is a decision you have to make; you can't allow your trouble to cause you to become bitter.

I ask you a question. If they had killed David, would that have brought back their family? Of course not. Would it have brought back their possessions? No.

It is interesting what bitterness can do to you. If you make somebody else's life miserable, is that going to change what happened to you? No. If you get revenge, is that going to change or stop what happened to you? No. If your heart gets full of intense hostility is that going to change what happened to you? No. Maybe you are in that place right now, I'm not judging you if you are. I'm just trying to show you how you can get out.

If bitterness is in your life, is it changing anything? Yes, it is. It is changing you! If you don't deal with it, starting now, in five years, 10 years, 15 years, there's not going to be anybody around you. People who love you right now are going to walk away from you. Do you know why? Because they are getting tired of getting blamed. They are getting tired of your hostility. They may love you, but they are going to love you at a distance because they are tired of you chunking rocks at them.

CHAPTER TWO

Charles, how do I get rid of it? You choose David's path. Are you ready? You go down David's path!

"David is greatly distressed; for the people spoke of stoning him because the soul of all the people was grieved, every man for his sons and his daughters; but David" –Did you see that? David chose a different path – "but David encouraged himself in the Lord, his God."

He didn't just encourage himself, no, no. This is way more than an emotional pep-talk. He encouraged himself in his relationship with the Lord. He went to the Lord. He went to the Lord, his God.

The word "Lord" is the Hebrew word "Yahweh," which means "Redeemer, Deliverer, Savior". He went to the part of the Godhead he knew as Redeemer, Deliverer, Savior. He went to who we know and who we call Jesus!

The word "God" used here is the Hebrew word "Elohim," which means The Trinity. He went to the Godhead and to the part of the Godhead he knew as Redeemer, Deliverer, Savior. Is that clear? He went to Him, and he encouraged himself in Him.

Please pay special attention to what I was going to share with you next. The word "encouraged" is very powerful. It means, number one, "to seize upon, to cleave, to fasten." When his men were looking for rocks and someone to blame, David went to the Lord, his God, and fastened himself to the Lord. He fastened himself to the Lord. I don't know any other way to say it to you. Please allow those words to paint an image in your mind of being fastened to the Lord. I think David was telling himself, "Bitterness is a no-win, destructive path. I am fastening myself to my Redeemer, my Deliverer, my Savior."

When life isn't playing along, one of the things that comes up in your mind is, "Is the Lord really here? Is he really going to help me?" That is why and when you have to fasten yourself to your Redeemer, Deliverer and Savior. You must turn your focus from your hurt and your pain to your Redeemer, Deliverer and Savior. You have to fasten yourself to Him and go to Him.

As I was going through this process, I want to share with you what happened to me. One night, I was lying in my bed, and I was having a terrible night. I'll be honest with you, it was a terrible night. It was 2:00 or 3:00 in the morning and I couldn't go to sleep. I was grieving and weeping and very sad and very lonely. I was thinking about the future and about everything Rochelle and I had done together and everything we had built together, and now I was going to finish the race without her. It was not what we had planned, it was not what we had dreamed, it was not what we had hoped, it was not what we had discussed. It was very sad for me. I was lying in my bed, and to be honest with you, I felt a little guilty that I was still here.

As I was lying there, and thinking about things, this thought came to me, "You've got to fasten yourself to Me. You've got to quit being attached to the past.

CHAPTER TWO

You have to fasten yourself to me." And then this thought came to me that is very powerful. Romans 12:15: "The gifts and the callings of God are without repentance."

I literally jumped up out of my bed, and I stood in my bedroom at 3:00 in the morning and lifted my hands toward heaven and said, "God, there's still a calling on my life. There is still a gift in my life, and that calling and that gift did not go away when Rochelle went away."

You see, you have a hope and a future (Jeremiah 29:11). You have a purpose and a calling. You were born with a plan that God has for your life. And whether people come or people go, that purpose remains in place. Let me say that again. That purpose, that calling, that plan, that hope, that future remains in place!

That same night, I made another vital decision about what road I was going to follow. I decided that what happened between Rochelle and the Lord was between Rochelle and the Lord, and what happens between me and the Lord is between me and the Lord. What happens between you and the Lord is between you and the Lord. And what happens between someone else in your life and the Lord is between them and the Lord.

I want to say this again, what happens between me and the Lord is between me and the Lord and has nothing to do with what happens between someone else and the Lord. It has everything to do with what happens between me and the Lord. The same is true for you.

"You were born with a plan that God has for your life. And whether people come or people go, that purpose remains in place."

I hope you will embrace this because there are things that happen to people and if you're not careful, you will begin to question your life in the light of what may have happened or did not happen with someone else. Does that make sense to you?

That was a great moment in my life. It was so liberating, so powerful, and so energizing. I was encouraging myself in the Lord. I hope that helps you. I was focusing on my relationship with Him. I wasn't looking to my own strength in any shape or form. I was looking to Him.

The last definition part of the word "encourage" means "to choose to be recovered." To choose to be recovered. Let's go back to David, in that moment. That day he was standing at a crossroads, he was surrounded by grieving men who had wept until they had no more power to weep.

Men whose souls were now bitter were looking for rocks to stone David. David came to the Lord, his

God, and fastened himself to his Redeemer, Deliverer and Savior. Because he was fastened to the Lord, his mindset became one that said, "Because I'm in this relationship with the Lord, I can do this. I choose, right here, right now, at this moment, I choose to be recovered! I'm not going to get recovered. I'm not going to be recovered. I'm not going to someday, by and by, get to recovery. No. Right here, right now, at this moment, I am — I choose to be recovered."

You can and must come to this same place in your life. You have got to come to the place in your life, in the Lord, where you say, "Jesus is here. Jesus is in me. Jesus is with me. And because of that, right here, right now, I choose to be recovered!" I've cried and I miss her, but I'm not going to grieve anymore. I choose to be recovered. Why? Because of Him.

If David can do this, you can do it.

If I can do this, you can do it too.

Isn't it interesting that thousands of years later, this same Yahweh, the same Messiah, shows up at the tomb of Lazarus and says, "I am the stand up. I am the recovery." He was then. He is now. And He will be 10,000 years from now. Anybody who wants to recover can recover. You don't have to do it. I'll do it for you. I will bring recovery to your life.

I decided that night in my bedroom. I chose to be recovered. I'm not going to get better, I am better. I chose to be recovered". Yes, I still miss her, but I can miss her and still be recovered.

Now, watch what happens in David's life. David begins to pray. That is a good thing to do. He seeks the Lord in verse **8**: "And David inquired at the Lord." He goes to Yahweh. He goes to the Redeemer, Deliverer and Savior saying, "Shall I pursue after this troop? Shall I overtake them?"

I want you to notice that David did not pray, "Lord, teach me how to cope." David said, "Because I'm recovered, I'm going to attack life. I'm going to attack life."

Shortly after this moment in my life, I began to tell everybody around me, "By the Lord's help, I'm going to attack life. I'm going to go after life. I'm going to live life with a vengeance. I am believing that my life will bear more fruit in the years I have left than all the fruit my life has borne up to this point."

"Shall I pursue? Shall I overtake?" Do you see, that is how a recovered man talks? There is life out there for me and you want me to go get it. I'm ready to go live. I am going to go get it."

Watch how the Lord answered David. What did David ask for? Two things, "Shall I pursue, and shall I overtake?" But He is the God that "does exceedingly abundantly above all you ask or think." (Ephesians 3:20)

God said, "Pursue, overtake. And without fail, recover all." David didn't think he could get it all back. He just wanted to go get even. God said, "I'm going to give you everything back. You chose to be recovered, so I am going to cause you to recover all."

CHAPTER TWO

I will be honest with you, in my life, I don't know what recovery fully means. I can't define it and I'm not trying to define it. I am not going to try to define to God what my recovery should be. Why should I want to define my recovery when He is the recovery? He is my stand up and my recovery. Why would I want to define what recovery should be? No, I am going to let Him define what my recovery is. But believe me, recovery is working in my life. It is operating in my life, and recovery is happening in my life.

Here is another truth I learned, and it has been absolutely life changing to me.

Revelation 1:8: Jesus said, "I am Alpha and Omega, the beginning and the ending, saith the Lord." This is Jesus talking.

What is Jesus? Alpha, Omega, beginning and ending. Alpha, Omega, beginning and ending. Jesus needs to be in your beginnings and in your endings, amen? Everything you begin, you want to begin it in Him. And anything that ends, you want it to end in Him.

One of the realities of life is that as we go through life, we have beginnings, and we have endings. All of us do. Jobs begin, jobs end. Relationships begin, relationships end.

Now, here is what is interesting. Jesus is, at the same time, in every moment, Jesus is Alpha and Omega in the same moment.

Think with me now. Think big. He is not Alpha, and then decides later to become Omega. No. He is Alpha Omega. He is beginning ending. He is in the same moment, He is both things. In your endings, He is also your new beginnings. When something ends, He is there to create a new beginning. He is there to give you a new beginning.

Look with me at Hebrews 12:2. It says, when he reveals to us that He is the author and the finisher of our faith. Author and finisher at the same time.

I want to tie two verses together with you.

Isaiah 14:17, God is speaking to satan, beginning in verse 12: "How thou art fallen from Heaven, O Lucifer, son of the morning. How you are cut down to the ground, which does weaken the nations. For you have said in your heart I will ascend into heaven, I will exalt my throne above the stars of God; I will also sit upon the mount of the congregation, in the sides of the north."

Verse 14: "I will ascend above the heights of the clouds; I will be like the most High God."

Pay close attention.

What does God say in Isaiah about satan's heart? He said, "satan wants to sit on the sides of the north. He wants to be on the mount of the congregation." He wants to sit on the sides of the north. He wants to exalt his throne above God's. He wants to be like the most high God. Did you catch all that?

CHAPTER TWO

Now let's look at Psalm 48:1: "Great is the Lord and greatly to be praised in the city of our God, in the mountain of his holiness."

The joy of the whole earth, is Mount Zion." Mount Zion, we know is the Old Testament name for the New Testament church. Do you see it?

Satan has always wanted to be the head of the church. He wanted to be the Lord of the congregation. He wanted to sit where the church sits. He wanted to rule the church. Not only rule the church, he wanted to be like the most high God.

Satan wants to sit in your endings. He wants to become Lord of your endings, instead of Jesus being the Lord of your endings. He wants your endings to be full of grief and pain and sorrow and bitterness and hurt and a sense of hopelessness and helplessness and no more future. That is what he wants to do. That is where he wants to sit. That is how he wants your endings to end, where he has camped and sat down. He wants to sit in the place where Jesus should be sitting. You need to tell him to get out of your endings and let Jesus come into your endings. You cannot let the devil fill your endings with pain and hurt. Instead, allow Jesus to come and bring you recovery and stand up and renewal and strength, so you can run and not be weary, walk and not faint. Don't let the devil usurp Jesus' position in your life!

I decided because Jesus is my Stand Up, my Recovery, my Life That Satisfies, my Alpha, my Omega, that satan was not going to be in my endings. If I can do it, you can do it.

How can we do that? Because He is the life that satisfies. He is our recovery. Let's pray together. Say this prayer out loud.

"Jesus, You are my stand up and my recovery. You are my Alpha and my Omega. You are in my beginnings, and You are in my endings. In every ending, there is a new beginning. I trust in Your ability to cause me to be recovered right here, right now. Right here, right now. In Your presence, I believe recovery is being released in my heart and mind. I believe that today, old books are closing, and new books are being opened. Lord, if a door has shut, I believe You are opening a new door. You are my Alpha and my Omega. You are my beginning and my ending. If there is an ending in my life, I know there is a new beginning starting, and I am looking for that new beginning. I'm not going to stand here and grieve over the door that closed. I am looking for the new door that You're opening because that is Your nature. You are my recovery."

Lord, I know there are people reading this book and praying with me that have lost people, things, relationships, opportunities, etc.; but I believe You are going to bring recovery, and we are going to let You define what the recovery is. We are not going to tell You what it is. We are going to let You define it. I am not the recovery. You are the recovery. But in You, I choose to be recovered, in Jesus' name.

As I was applying the truths — Jesus being our Stand Up and Recovery — there was another great revelation that came to my heart.

One day, during my devotional time, I felt like the Lord spoke to me and said, "I want you to get all of the fruit you can out of the fields and trees that are already producing fruit in your life. Get all you can." The idea being, there is fruit that God wants us to bear. John 15, Jesus says, "My father cleanses every branch, so it can bring forth mega fruit," and the more fruit our lives bear, John 15:8 says, the more glory God receives.

As His disciples, our lives are to bear fruit, and not just some fruit, MEGA FRUIT. It is God's spoken will for your life and my life that our lives bear mega fruit, and yet in bearing this mega fruit, there are times when we, leave fruit in the field. This is especially true if you have taken a major hit in your life, like I did with Rochelle's passing. I think it is only natural to lose your energy and expectations about what your life can be and what you can accomplish, after going through a traumatic event, especially if you are not focused or you step into survivor mode.

Looking back, I can see how the Lord used this statement to cause me to focus on my present and future life, and not get bogged down in the past. The thought of leaving fruit in the fields, or on the trees, really bothered me. I have always diligently tried to be a good steward of what the Lord had given me. Of course, this would include my life happening in the present and going forward.

Why did this become so important to me and why can it be important to you? After you go through a life-hit, if you are not careful, you can begin to coast through your life, your relationships, your career. This is possible even if you didn't take a life-hit because you begin to settle for "just enough" life. Just enough fruit to make it, to survive. We can fall into this mindset subconsciously.

I want to challenge you, before we go any further, to do a real evaluation of you, your life, your relationships, your health, your finances, your career, and ask yourself, "Am I leaving fruit in the fields?"

If you own a business, I encourage you to really look at your business and ask, "Are we leaving fruit in the field?" Is there profit for you to make that you're not making because you haven't seen it, or you haven't thought about it? Or was there profit you were making, but now, as the Song of Solomon 2:15 says, the little foxes have come in and are stealing the fruit off your vine.

Maybe there is a relationship that could bear more fruit. How many times relationships do not blossom or produce the full fruit that they could? A husband-and-wife relationship, friendship relationships, how many of them don't produce the way God wants them to produce because we don't look for all the fruit that can be there? We miss some of the fruit. The little foxes come in and steal the fruit off the vine.

I began to focus on this, and I began thinking about my life and my church. I began to look at all of my relationships with my friends. I became more serious about my personal health, my fitness, my diet, other things, because God had spoken to me about not leaving harvest in the fields, and about getting all the fruit I could out of my life.

That sounds a little covetous, and I hope you don't take it that way. It is not about getting all I can get. No. It is about producing all of the fruit that God has placed in my life to produce, to His glory.

Matthew 13. In this chapter, Jesus teaches back-to-back-to-back parables, and then He explains one of the parables. Let's go to the explanation. Verse 37: "He answered and said unto them, He that soweth the good seed is the Son of Man."

What does Jesus sow? Good seed. Please understand that Jesus' relationship with you and me is all about Him sowing good seed into your life. In Mark 4, He referred to Himself as the sower sowing the Word. "So the sower sows the word." So, the good seed that Jesus sows into your life and my life is the Word.

That is a micro view of your relationship. Then He expands His explanation into a macro view of the world.

"He that soweth the good seed is the Son of Man. The field is the world. The good seed are the children of the kingdom."

He sows His Word into me and you, and then He sows us into the world. What does He want us to do in the world? Bear fruit. "So shall you be my disciples, bear fruit." Live fruitful lives. How? By the Word producing in your life. The Word leading you, guiding you, renewing your mind, building faith in your heart, causing you to make right, life-producing choices.

"The field is the world. The good seed are the children of the kingdom, but the tares are the children of the wicked one." In the parable, before the explanation, Jesus said that the farmer went out and sowed wheat, and then an enemy came and sowed tares. And He said that the tares are the children of the wicked.

In a macro view, a world view, what we have in society today is what we've had ever since Jesus came. We have the children of the kingdom living their lives and the children of the wicked living their lives. And they could literally grow up next door to each other.

A lot of times, we, as children of God, ask, "Why is evil allowed to stay here?" I don't know why He doesn't take them out, but He doesn't. He let's the good seed and the tares grow together. I think it's because He has the ability to turn a tare into a wheat. That happens as we let our light shine and as we bear the right fruit, people see that fruit, and they begin to ask, "What's going on? Look at you and look at us. How can I get that kind of fruit or harvest in my life which can bring about change?"

The tares are the children of the wicked one. We also see this in Mark 4:13-20. While the good seed is being sown, satan comes and sows because he wants to steal the Word. He wants to take the Word of God out of your life or get you to walk away from the Word of God, to abandon the Word of God because of persecution and affliction, through being hard-hearted, through the cares of this world, lusts of other things, deceitfulness of riches, entering into our hearts and choking the Word, and it becomes unfruitful causing you to become offended. All of this comes to fight for your harvest. The enemy that sowed them is the devil, verse 39. The harvest is the end of the world and the reapers are the angels.

I want us to focus on verse 39, "The harvest is the end." So, the enemy wants to affect the end. He sows all the bad seed for the purpose of affecting "the ending." Satan wants to affect our endings. I believe with all my heart that you and I need to take heed to what we are listening to and to what we are allowing into our circle of influence. We need to be aware of how we handle and take care of our fields so satan can't accomplish his goal of stealing some of our fruit.

Verse 41: "So the Son of Man shall send forth His angels. They shall gather out of His kingdom all things that offend and them which do iniquity."

The tares are sown, and when the reapers come, they take the tares out. Jesus said that the tares, which are things that you and I need to be careful of in our lives, can be classified in two ways, things that offend and iniquity.

In my life, if I am going to get all the fruit that God wants me to get out of my field, whether it is the field of pastoring, whether it is the field of being a dad or a grandparent or a friend or as a disciple, or my relationship with God, there are two things I need to watch out for. Number one is that I don't allow myself to live an offended life.

I don't think Jesus is talking about being offended occasionally. I was in a restaurant one time, and a couple of tables over from me, some men were talking and one of them said something really foul. To be honest with you, it offended me, but I'm not offended now. I wanted to take him home and wash his mouth out with soap. That's what he needed. Be aware, there is a difference between being offended for a moment and living an offended lifestyle. An offended lifestyle is to the extent where a person wakes up offended, he goes to work offended, he gets in the car and knows somebody is going to offend him while driving. Do you live an offended life?

The word "offended" in the Greek language has a three-fold progressive definition. We don't have this kind of definition in English. The Greek language describes three steps to being offended. Number one, you become displeased, and you begin to live a displeased life. There is possibly a few of you reading this book and you are living a displeased life. I see them come to our church, they are sitting in a beautiful sanctuary, surrounded by people who are going out of their way to be nice, kind, helpful, encouraging; and yet, they are displeased. It could be anything that irritates a person living a displeased life. The music is too loud or isn't loud enough. There are too many lights, not enough lights. It's too hot, too cold, "too" something. The person behind you is breathing too loud. They are offended and displeased because the pastor doesn't have on a suit or is wearing expensive shoes. Again, I'm not talking about being displeased occasionally or momentarily. I'm talking about living a displeased lifestyle. Being displeased with your spouse, your family, your neighbors, the people you work with, total strangers! Being displeased is your vibe, it is the atmosphere you create and carry with you. I know it doesn't sound like it should be such a big deal, but it is because over time displeasure evolves into the next step, which is more destructive and life-crushing.

The second step is displeasure morphing into resentment. I challenge you to look around and observe the lives of people you know, and you might see it. Not everybody, but there are a lot of people in our world today who live offended lives. They become displeased about something, they never dealt with it, and now they are resentful.

It amazes me how many people live resentful lives. They live angry lives because someone insulted them or hurt them in some way. Now, they are not only angry at the person and institution that hurt them or insulted them, they are angry all the time, even with people that had nothing to do with the original offense. I have been around displeased, resentful people – not fun. Sadly, some of them don't realize how satan is stealing the good fruit from their lives and poisoning their lives at the same time.

Ultimately, satan wants to get us to progress to the third step: that you fall back into your sinful ways and you become bitter. We need to be on guard. I have seen this happen so many times. Someone becomes displeased, they don't deal with it, over time, displeasure grows into resentment, they don't deal with, and resentment grows into full-on offense, and they fall into sin, becoming bitter.

This can happen very easily if your life takes a body shot like mine did. Thankfully, when Rochelle died, I knew satan would try to cause me to become offended. I knew he would start with displeasure. "This should not have happened. We are good people. We serve God. We go to church. I'm upset she isn't with me." If I had gone down that path, displeasure would have grown into resentment. My anger would have taken over my life. I would have begun to lash out at people and life in general. I could have justified my resentment. I could have given in to sin and bitterness. That is not what I want, and I don't think you do either. We cannot allow satan to sow the tare of being offended into our fields.

Jesus also showed us there is a second tare that satan wants to sow into our fields (our hearts and souls), the tare of iniquity. The Bible dictionary defines "iniquity" as "lawlessness." In scripture, "lawless" does not mean disobeying natural law or laws in the country or the society you live in. God deals on a higher level than that. He defines lawlessness as rebelling against God's instruction. We reject God's instruction. That becomes your lifestyle. We live a lifestyle of lawlessness, or we live a lifestyle of rejecting God's instruction.

In the original text, the definition carries with it the idea that it is not only rejecting instruction that God has specifically said not to do or to do, but also instruction that the Bible does not specifically contain. The Bible does not contain every instruction for every possible contingency of your life. It can't. It would be so big you wouldn't be able to get anything out of it. There are 8 billion people on the planet. If God had one book that covered every person, no one could use the book. So, what does He do? God writes His Word, His laws, on your heart.

Let's talk about this. There are things the Bible does not specifically address, but you know in your heart those things are wrong for you. To reject that is lawlessness. It is not just the written commands. It is the commands on your heart. I think you and I can see if I reject His instructions, especially the ones written on my heart, that is going to stop me from getting all the fruit out of my life God wants me to get. In fact, it may take me right out of the field where the fruit is growing!

We are supposed to live fruitful lives. We understand fruit carries with it the idea of a beginning and an ending – seed time and harvest time – beginning and ending. Every spring, farmers around the world will begin. In the fall, they will end. There will be seed time and harvest. The fact there is a harvest reinforces the fact there is an ending. Yet, with the end, there is the promise of a new beginning!

I used to have a friend who had a beautiful peach farm in South Carolina. He ruined me because he allowed me to eat real peaches. Peaches that were left on the tree until they were so ripe you couldn't believe it. Peaches that were as big as softballs. He would leave some of them on the trees and then let his friends go out and pick them. You would barely touch the peaches and they would come off the tree. When you bit into them, you had to lean over to avoid being covered in peach juice. They tasted like they were injected with pure sugar, they were so sweet and so beautiful. Oh, my Lord, I'm hungry for one of those peaches! I always used to figure out a way to get an invitation to come speak at his church right around harvest time. It was a sad day for me when he sold the farm and retired.

Later, I learned that they would let the harvesters go through with instructions to leave a certain percentage of the peaches on the top of the trees. So the pickers would pick on the bottom, leaving some of the peaches to stay longer. Then, before he let his friends into the fields, he and his family — the father, the mother, and the children — would go through the fields and pick the best peaches. They would take those to their house and take the seeds out. In his house, he had a protected area where he kept all those seeds.

One year, I asked him, "Pete, why do you do that?" He explained if for some reason he lost his fields, he would still have the best seeds that the trees ever produced, and he could start over.

You see, with every harvest there is an end, but in that ending, there is the promise of a new beginning. Let me continue with this thought. Life, my life, your life, is full of endings. Every day ends, every year ends; but, with the ending is the promise of a new beginning! Life is full of endings. Many times in life, eras end, relationships end.

Sometimes the endings are expected and sometimes they're not. I expect every year to end. It doesn't surprise me. I expect each day to end. Sometimes, endings are gradual, like a school year. Sometimes endings are abrupt, like when someone passes away that you didn't expect, or when a friendship ends abruptly. Even successful businesses can end gradually or seemingly overnight. For example, great fortunes were made years ago on whale oil until Edison figured out how to run electricity down the streets. The whale oil business ended, bankrupt, gone. Endings can come abruptly in the form of a bankruptcy, a divorce, a job that ends, a partnership that dissolves. The list goes on and on.

Sometimes it is just time to put an end to something. But the reality is, I think that we, as a species are fearful of endings. We don't like them. We don't like to talk about them, but life is full of them.

John 19:28 "After this, Jesus, knowing that all things were now accomplished (or coming to an end), that the Scripture might be fulfilled, said, 'I thirst'. Now there was set a vessel full of vinegar -- and they filled a sponge with vinegar and put it upon a hyssop (or sponge), and put it to His mouth. When Jesus, therefore, had received the vinegar, He said, 'It is finished', and He bowed His head and gave up the ghost."

One translation says, "He gave up His spirit."

I want to point something out to you. "It" came to an end, but He did not. He said, "It is finished." He didn't say, "I am finished."

Often times all of us have "its" that finish, but that doesn't mean you're finished. "It" may finish. "It" maybe an era, a relationship, something in your life. It may finish, but that doesn't mean you're finished. You've got to be careful in your life that you don't see the end of an assignment as the end of your destiny or the end of a relationship as the end of your life and happiness. I have looked back on my life, and I can see all kinds of times where "it" finished. Because "it" finished doesn't mean I finished, or because "it" finished doesn't mean you're finished. Satan will try to make you think that "it" is you, and if "it" ends, you're done. But "it" can end and you're not done.

He gave up His spirit, but He didn't give up! In fact, He was just getting started.

We must understand this about life, because "it" is finished, you are not finished. There is a big difference, as I said, between the end of an era or the end of assignment and the completion of your destiny. The end of a relationship is not the end of your life! Understanding this truth when Rochelle passed away energized me.

Philippians 1:6, "Being confident of this very thing" – we need to be confident of this very thing – "that he which has begun a good work" (beginning). "He which has begun a good work in you will perform it until the day of Jesus Christ." (ending).

As you are reading this book, without knowing you, I can say, sometime in your life, Jesus began a good work in you and He is continuing to do that good work in your life. He will continue to do that good work in your life as you go through beginnings and endings, endings and beginnings, in every stage of your life. He will not stop until He comes back or you go to Him!

"Be confident in this," put your confidence in this, that "it" may finish, but He is not finished with you!

CHAPTER THREE

You may be reading this book and recently the devil has been telling you, "You're old now, God's through with you." God is not through with you, not until you go to Him or He comes for you. Until then, you have an assignment. You have a purpose. You've got something that He still has on your plate.

Maybe you are sitting at your house, and all you are thinking about is what used to be...you need to quit doing that. The devil is robbing you of the fruit that is in your field, that God still wants you to harvest.

Maybe you are reading this book and recently, you lost your significant other, and now you are walking around saying, "I can't live. I don't have any reason to live. I wish I could die." Please don't allow that thinking to persist. "It" ended. "It" ended, but you didn't!

Jesus gave up the spirit, but He didn't give up. That is spectacular! Unless it is the day when He comes for you or you go to Him, then you are not finished in life!

Endings can be God-given opportunities. Most people don't know how to handle endings. I will tell you a couple of funny things I have seen.

I travel a lot. One of the funniest things I see when I travel is how some people walk through airports. In DFW airport, London Heathrow, all of the big airports I go through, there are two flows, right? We divide like we do on the streets. I think it's one of the funniest things we do as humans. We move over to one side. Now, in London, my tendency is to go right, but there I have to move over to the left side.

Another funny thing is when some people will be walking and everybody is walking behind them and they just stop, totally oblivious to the chaos that they have just created behind them. Have you seen this one? Someone is driving, and they just stop. They don't know where they're supposed to go now. The road dead ends and they need to go right or left, but they just stop,and everybody behind them start slamming on their brakes. Everyone is backing up behind them because they are supposed to go to the right or to the left. No. They just stop because they don't know how to handle endings.

I was in the Dallas airport one time. They have huge escalators. Maybe you have seen them. When you are going up to the tram in the American Airlines terminal, there are huge escalators that go up very steeply. I don't know how tall they are. They go up and up and up, and on the escalators, there are dozens of people. Everyone is standing with all their carry-on bags. Way up at the top, there is mom and dad, and they're coming up to the end. You can tell they have never been on this escalator before, and as soon as the escalator comes to the end, they take the smallest of steps and stop. There is absolute chaos behind them on the escalator because people have nowhere to go. Mom, dad, you must keep walking. The escalator ended, but you can't stop.

We are having fun with this, but it proves a point. People don't know what to do when things come to an end. The result is oftentimes chaos because they don't know what to do. Why? When we get to the end, we are not supposed to stop. It is almost too simple.

CHAPTER THREE

"The end of an era is not the completion of a destiny."

Jesus is the beginning and the ending. He specializes in endings. He called Himself Alpha and Omega, beginning and ending. He specializes in beginnings, and He specializes in endings.

Beginnings, in fact, come from endings. That is the fact of a harvest. I get a new harvest because I had an old harvest (ending). A harvest is the ending of a beginning, and this ending produces a beginning.

Please listen carefully.

Satan will try to affect or sit in your endings, thereby stopping you from sowing the new seed for your new beginning. Satan will try to plant his tares where good seed was supposed to go. He will try to come in and plant tares, such as worry, offense, lawlessness, rebellion, cares of this world, deceitfulness of riches, lusts of other things. He will try to plant his tares in your good field to rob you of your harvest.

The harvest comes from the new seed sown in your life. Satan will try to rob you of the new harvest at the end of something through guilt, regret, loss of interest in life, grief, shame, etc.

Let me say it to you again. The end of an era is not the completion of a destiny. "He that begins a good work in you will complete it." You are not complete until you go to Him, or He comes for you.

One of the most common and destructive tares is regret. The dictionary defines regret as "pain of mind on account of something done or experienced in the past with the wish it had been different." Do you know what regret does? Regret holds us in neutral. It puts us in neutral, so we are not going forward. It causes us to try to fix what can't be fixed. Trust me on this. I know a little bit about this. If trying to fix what you can't fix, your mind will go like a buzz saw; but, you can't undo what happened. All you can do is learn from it and go plant your new seed and not allow the devil to steal out of that new field like he stole out of that old field. Nothing creates regret like endings.

Hebrews 3:14, "For we are made partakers of Christ." Don't you love that? Partakers of Christ. "For we are made partakers of Christ if we hold the beginning of our confidence steadfast unto the end." Holding steadfast, from beginning to ending.

The word "holding" means "to retain." The antonym means "to give up or surrender." Don't give up. Because you came to an ending, don't give up. Don't surrender. See a new beginning. Become indignant. Get your roar back! Where is your new beginning? Jesus is your new beginning!

CHAPTER THREE

I know, you didn't want the ending. I know, I didn't want the ending either and got it anyway. It doesn't matter. The end came. So, where is the new beginning? You may have prayed against this end. So did I. The end came. Where is your new beginning? The devil is going to try to rob your steadfast confidence. He wants you to give up and surrender; but, you are not going to give and surrender. I'm not going to let you give up and surrender. I'm going to keep speaking to you until you get off the ground!

He said to hold fast your confidence. The word "confidence" means your "hope." And what is hope? Hope is positive expectation. What is positive expectation in the light of what we are learning? To me, it sounds like this:

> Is there a harvest coming for me? Is there a new beginning coming for me? With that new beginning is a new harvest. I don't understand what happened, but there is a new beginning for me. My life isn't over. Your life isn't over. "It" came to an end, but you didn't come to an end! You may have just finished a season that has left a taste of bitter, sour wine in your mouth, but you didn't end. "It" ended.

Jesus died with sour wine in His mouth, but He didn't end! "It" ended.

That is spectacular. He said, "Hold fast your hope, be steadfast." Steadfast means "that which you are building until the end." The word end literally means "when there is no more time."

"It" ended, but I did not end!

"How long do I have to hold on, Pastor?" Until there is no more time. This is God's view over your life. I ask you, look up! Your life is not over. Yes, you may have experienced an ending you were not ready for, but, say it with me — "It" ended, but I did not end!

I encourage you today. Give yourself permission to live, dream again. Allow yourself to love, laugh, have fun. God's hope and future for you has not ended!

In society, we are programmed to think in this order, beginnings and endings, nothing wrong with that, but I want us to focus on the transverse: endings and beginnings.

One of the ingredients of life is endings and beginnings.

Matthew 13, in the parable of the good seed and the bad seed, the parable of the wheat and the tares, one of the things that satan tries to do is when Jesus sows good seed into your life, he tries to sow bad seed right next to the good seed because he wants to affect your endings. Why? Because satan knows, oftentimes in life, we are not prepared for endings. We are not ready for them.

I told you that oftentimes you will see people driving in their car and the street will come to an end and they're not prepared for it and they just stop. And then what happens behind them? Chaos.

CHAPTER FOUR

Not very long ago, I was at a mall in our city, and I was on the escalator. There were people in front of me, and we're riding up, and it was crowded behind me. We got to the top of the escalator and some people just stopped. They took the smallest of steps and stopped, but the escalator doesn't stop. People were backing up and someone said, "Geez, lady, move, because we have nowhere to go." My point being is that, obviously, they weren't ready for the end. If you're not ready for the end, chaos can come into your life and the lives of people you are connected with.

Jesus said, "I am the beginning and the ending." He wants to sit in our endings, but satan wants to usurp Jesus' position and sit in our endings instead. If we don't understand endings and we don't understand what they are and how to respond to them, then we cannot go forward or get our new beginning. You may know someone right now who is stuck in an ending. As a result, their life is not progressing. They are not going forward.

Life is full of endings. Sometimes it is expected and sometimes it's abrupt; but, we get fearful of endings.

I want to remind you of what we just looked at in John 19 where Jesus was on the cross and He gave up His spirit. And then He said, "It is finished." The important thing to remember is that "it" was finished, but He was not finished.

An era may end, but your purpose does not. Something in your life may come to an end, but you don't end.

Jesus gave up His spirit, but He did not give up. "It" ended, but He did not end. A couple of verses later, they came to break His legs, which they didn't do. They didn't break Him either. His purpose continued. "It" was finished, but He was not.

Endings can be God-given opportunity to get a new beginning. Many people don't know how to handle endings, and because they don't, then their lives go into chaos. Why? When you get to the end, you are not supposed to stop. Your Savior specializes in endings!

Look at Hebrews 3:14 again, "For we are made partakers of Christ if we hold the beginning of our confidence steadfast unto the end." If we hold the beginning of our confidence steadfast to the end — from beginning to end.

What I have found in life – and I'm sure you have too – is that life will try to beat your confidence down to the ground. Life tries to cause you to lose or let go of your confidence. The Holy Spirit tells us to hold fast to our confidence. Remember, the word "confidence" means "hold fast to what you are building." So, you are building your purpose, your destiny in God, and God is building something in your life, and even though endings come, and things happen we don't like or understand, we are to hold fast to our confidence. Even though life is trying to beat that confidence out of us, we are to hold fast to our confidence. It is up to me to hold fast to my steadfast confidence.

CHAPTER FOUR

As you go through life, "it" may be finished, but you are not finished. "It" may be an era in your life, a relationship in your life, those things end, but you do not.

Like you, many times I have had things and relationships that I thought, quite honestly, would continue for all my life, and the thing or the relationship came to an end. But you can't stop there.

A lot of people do get stopped. They stop. They are on the escalator, the escalator ends, and they stop. They are on the road, the road ends, and they stop. You cannot stop. You've got to go right, you've got to go left, but you've got to go. You can't park. You cannot stop!

I have had things, relationships, et cetera, that I thought would always continue, and they or "it" came to an end. Jesus said, "It is finished," but He was not. In truth, He was just beginning. So "it" ends. Yet, these "its" in my life have ended, and still a new beginning came to pass by holding fast to my confidence, steadfast, unto the end. To get through an ending, you have to be committed to what is on the other side. You can't hold on to the old and live the rest of your life in regret.

When I was writing this book and thinking about it, the Lord brought a memory back to me. Several years ago, I was speaking for a really good friend of mine in Oslo, Norway. One night when the conference was over, they took me into the city. They said, "We want to take you to a really cool restaurant." I said, "Great, I love cool restaurants." So they took me and it was really cool. When we were done eating, we drove around the restaurant, and up a hill and parked. It was in January. It was freezing. They asked me to get out of the car. I said, "I don't really want to." I don't like cold weather. They said, "No. You're going to want to." We got out of the car, and we walked across ice, and I realized we were in an arena of some type, a big place, outdoor place, a stadium.

The national sport of Norway is ski jumping. They are the gold medal winners, favorites every year, every Olympics. We were at the national ski jump stadium, but we were at the top, looking down the ramp. The stadium seats a hundred thousand people. I was almost hyperventilating just looking at it and thinking, "You have to be certifiably crazy to get on skis and go down this jump." It's amazing to watch on television. You can't imagine standing up there and looking at it.

I looked at the pastor, and said, "How do you do this the first time?" He said to me, "Charles, you just have to commit to it." They have a saying in skiing: "When you get up on the mountain, you have to commit to the mountain." You've got to commit.

When you come to an ending, you have to commit to what's on the other side. There is another side. He is the beginning and ending. He is your stand up and recovery. He is ending and beginning. There is a beginning. There is something else on the other side, and you've got to commit to it. You have to commit to what's on the other side of that ending because that is a part of your stand up and your recovery.

CHAPTER FOUR

"When you come to an ending, you have to commit to what's on the other side."

I want to talk to you about taking responsibilities for endings. There are five truths I've found in my life and studying other people that you need to focus on when endings come.

Number one, you need to believe the best for your future. My prayer is that you and I, when we are 95 years old, will get up in the morning and say, "The best is yet to come." Instead of being the grouchy old people that talks about how great it was in 1938. Who cares what it was like in '38? In 1938, they had no outdoor plumbing, no or very little electricity, hardly any good medicine, no vaccines. It wasn't that good. I like living today. So, you don't want to become that grouchy old guy or the grouchy old lady?

Believe the best for your future. You know why that is good? It is because it stops the ending from ruling you.

Most people know Jeremiah 29:11. If you don't know it, you'll recognize it when you read it. Jeremiah

29:11, "For I know the thoughts I think toward you, sayeth the Lord, thoughts of peace and not of evil, to give you a future and a hope." To give you a future and a hope.

A lot of people know that verse. We are acquainted with it. It's beautiful. We confess it over our lives. We hold onto it, that God is thinking these thoughts toward us.

Let me tell you the context. When God wrote this to the Nation of Israel through the prophet Jeremiah, the Nation of Israel was in captivity in Babylon. They were mourning that they had lost Jerusalem. Remember, for all of the Jews, all of their hope all the time was in Jerusalem. "If we could just be in Jerusalem. Life will be better if we were just in Jerusalem."

But they had been hauled into captivity, into Babylon. As far as they knew, they had come to an unexpected, horrible end, and God has Jeremiah write them a letter.

So, they are at an end that could have ended their existence and their confidence, but in Verse 4 He writes to them, "Thus sayeth the Lord of Hosts, the God of Israel, unto all that are carried away captive who I have caused to be carried into exile from Jerusalem unto Babylon."

They are in captivity. Life as they thought it was going to be ended, but look what God tells them to do from these scriptures, "Build houses, dwell in them; plant gardens and eat the fruit of them; take wives and have sons and daughters; and take wives for your sons and give your daughters to husbands that they may bear sons and daughters, that you may be increased and not diminished."

They thought they had no future, and God reminded them that they had a great future. Even though you had an ending, take your eyes off it. Quit looking back at Jerusalem. Start building houses and planting gardens and growing vineyards and having kids and getting married. Your future is good. God says "I'm thinking good thoughts toward you." I love this.

When an ending comes in your life, number one, believe that the best is yet to come. Truth number two to focus on when endings come, talk to your future. Psalm 23:6 says: "Surely, goodness and mercy shall follow me all the days of my life." David is talking to his future. Do you hear him? "Surely, goodness and mercy will follow me all the days of my life, and I will dwell in the house of the Lord forever." What is David doing? He is speaking to his future. He is committed to the other side. He is committed to the other side of the ending. He is speaking to it. He is declaring it and talking to it.

Truth number three, commit to the future. If something is over, you can't keep holding onto it or your life will begin to stink. You can't keep holding onto "it."

What causes people to hold onto something that is over? Regrets and offenses. Don't hold onto them. Proverbs 4:23 says you need "to guard your heart with all diligence for out of it come the boundaries of your life." So, commit to the future.

One of the songs we sing at church says, "I don't have time to maintain these regrets." I love that song. You can't hold onto it. If it's over, it's over. Don't hold onto it anymore. Remember, "it" is over, you are not. Jesus is bringing stand up and recovery to your life.

Truth number four to remember when endings come, keep yourself fresh. When an ending comes, keep yourself fresh. What do I mean by that? Ecclesiastes 10:10, "If the iron be blunt and he did not sharpen the edge, then he must put more strength to it." He is talking about an axe. If the axe is blunt, then you have to swing it harder. You've got to use more effort with less results.

I know in my own life, sometimes when I came to an ending in my life, I tend to get tired. Endings are exhausting. They are draining. They can drain everything out of you. I end up pushing more and working harder, but I am not getting as much fruit. I end up pushing the people around me more, and they are not bearing as much fruit. As a result, we are leaving fruit in the fields.

I need to refresh myself, and I need to back up and look at myself and quit thinking old thoughts and get new thoughts and look at things a new way and read some new books. I need to hang around people who are not at the end, who are in a beginning, and get that energy back and get around people who are doing things.

CHAPTER FOUR

You can't just sit up at the house and cry or drive around town mad or look for his car so you can key it. What is wrong with you? You have to keep yourself fresh.

Truth number five, this may be one of the most important truths I will say to you in this book. Never allow your faith to come down to the level of your experience.

II Corinthians 4:13 says we have the same spirit of faith. Maintain your faith. Don't let it come down to the level of your experience. Don't change your view of the abundant life because you've come to an end you didn't expect. Keep your faith above it and maintain your faith at that level and don't let it come down to the level of your experience.

I met a man years ago, an incredible man of God. He was a real friend to me in my city. When we first got started, I didn't have a lot of pastors who wanted to be my friend, but he was my friend. We were talking one time, and he said to me, "I came to one of your services."

I said, "I wish I would have known."

He said, "Yes, I came, and I saw that you and your church were praying for the sick."

I said, "Yes, we do that."

He said, "I don't believe in that anymore."

I said, "Why not?"

"In life, you are either making things happen or you're letting things happen, but things are happening."

"My wife got real sick one time and she didn't get better. So, I don't believe in healing anymore."

I'm not judging him. My point is that what happened to him was his faith came down to the level of his experience. If that happens to you, then you are not going to recover. You are not going to have what Jesus wants you to have. This, to me, is the real battle. The real battle is over your faith. Satan wants to rob you of your faith so you don't have the life God wants you to have. You've got to commit to the other side of the ending and maintain your faith and have that spirit of faith. I believe that I need to, and you need to take responsibility for endings. When an ending comes, we must take responsibility. We must address it and engage it. We cannot ignore it.

In life, you are either making things happen or you're letting things happen, but things are happening. It is one or the other. I believe one of the most important things we can do when we come to an ending is have a confident expectation regarding the ending.

I want to show you David having a bad day from Psalm 142. David was acquainted with bad days. Some of them he created, and others were the result of decisions others made. This is a bad day that someone else created.

David wrote this psalm when he was living in a cave, hiding from Saul. He was anointed to be king, he had killed Goliath, and he was living in a cave. This made life as a shepherd look pretty good.

And he writes: "I cried unto the Lord with my voice, with my voice unto the Lord that I make my supplication. I poured out my complaint before him and I showed before him my trouble."

He was saying, "I've got things to complain about and I've got troubles."

"When my spirit was overwhelmed within me."

He was overwhelmed by his troubles.

"Then you knew my path. In the way wherein I walked have they privately laid a snare for me."

Do you know what I'm saying? "They're out to get me." Have you ever had that feeling? "They're out to get me." I've had that feeling.

Verse 4: "I looked to my right hand and behold, there was no man that would know me."

So, he said, "I'm in this hard place and no one will acknowledge me. I never get the credit. No one wants to help me."

I wonder if you have ever been frustrated with never getting the credit and always getting the blame. If so, perhaps you could have written Psalm 142.

He's not done: "Refuge failed me. No man cared for my soul."

Refuge failed me. He is saying he has no place to hide. Nowhere to go. No one who cares for his soul. There is no one to help him. I think David could have added that he helped a lot of people, but no one is helping him. Ever felt that way?

Watch him. He begins to turn, saying, "I cried unto you, O, Lord. I said you are my refuge and my portion in the land of the living."

He previously said nobody cares for me and everybody is against me. All that negative mentality, and then he got his focus. He said, Lord, You care for me and You will be my refuge. "You'll be my portion in the land of the living." He bounces back. This is real life right here. This is a man talking to his future. He is committed to what is on the other side of his ending. He knows with the Lord on his side this needing will not end in an ending, but he will get his new beginning.

CHAPTER FOUR

He said, "Attend unto my cry for I am brought very low."

We could say David was battling depression. "I am brought very low."

"Deliver me from my persecutors for they are stronger than I. Bring me out of prison that I may praise Your name. The righteous shall compass me about for You have dealt bountifully with me."

He was having a lousy day, but he said it is going to get better. You are going to deal "bountifully with me." He committed to the other side. He begins to turn around. His confident expectation came back. He began to speak to his future. He didn't accept inevitability, which is a mistake many of us make. The phrase we use is: whatever will be will be. Really?

I believe that destiny is about purpose and not about fate. God said, "I have a purpose for you." It is not about fate. It is about purpose.

Satan will try to plant his tares where Jesus has planted His good seeds in your life, good seeds of faith, good seeds of hope, good seeds of confidence. Satan will try to plant doubt and fear and unbelief and depression and hopelessness. He will try to plant his bad seed right next to the good seed.

Where are you sitting right now? It may be hard for you to accept that on the other side of this ending there can be something better. It may be hard for you to accept until you realize God has a purpose for your life, and when "it" ended, your purpose didn't. You can stand up with a faith and hope that you are going to recover all. Purpose doesn't end until you go to Jesus or Jesus comes to you. What is even more spectacular is when you understand that the end may end up being better than the beginning.

Again, we can't go through life letting life happen to us. Here is an amazing verse of scripture. Ecclesiastes 7:8, Solomon writes, "Better is the end of a thing than the beginning."

Better is the end of a thing than the beginning. You know what that verse gives me? Confident expectation of what is on the other side of my endings. That verse will cause your faith to influence your actions. When we take responsibility for endings, you will live life with a different spirit. You will approach life differently.

Psalm 119:12 says, "I've inclined my heart to perform your statutes always, even unto the end."

This is a man that wasn't afraid of the end. He was saying, I'm here for the long haul. I'm going all the way through to the end.

"Hold fast your steadfast confidence and then you will partake of everything Christ has for you."

Most of us, when we think of an ending, we think of the big ending, eternity. Hopefully, you are not afraid of the end of life. You have already accepted Jesus as Lord and the end of life doesn't concern you because you know when your time comes, to be absent from your body is to be present with the Lord (II Corinthians 5:8).

But what about all the other endings in your life? He is saying the Word takes you through those endings. It takes you forward.

There are three realities that come when you accept responsibility for your ending.

Number one, the first thing you wll discover is a burst of new ideas, new dreams, creativity will come into your life when you are committed to the other side, the new beginning.

When Rochelle passed away, good Lord, that was an ending I wasn't even ready for. I had never gone there mentally. I wouldn't allow myself to go there emotionally. But then, there it was. It wasn't an ending I chose. It isn't an ending any of us chooses. Yet, there it was.

That is when I began to study, and what I found over the next two years became some of the most important truths of my life. Truths that empowered me, my family, our church and thousands of other people.

I believe creativity comes when you see the ending as a chance for a new beginning, when you see Jesus in that ending and you are committed to the other side of it and you just don't stop. You don't pull over. You don't park.

"I have no reason to live." What are you talking about? You have no reason to live? Maybe you need to hear this. You may be walking around believing the end of your relationship means the end of your life. You have no reason to live? Are you kidding me, you have no reason to live?

I know I just made you mad, but good. Maybe I will make you so mad you won't be able to sleep tonight, and you will start praying. Then God can speak to you and get you out of that thinking because the devil is robbing you. What do you mean you have no reason to live? There are people in hospitals all around you who are fighting to live, and you are sitting there saying you don't have any reason to live? Stop allowing the devil to put that tare in your mind! Let's pull it out right now and commit to the other side of your ending. Commit to your stand up and your recovery and get ready for creativity to burst forth into your life. Your life is going to get better.

A lot of times endings force you to create. Don't just surrender to the end. Think creatively. Don't accept limitations as final. I am telling you, endings can force creativity and innovation in your life.

Reality number two: new vision will come when you accept responsibility for endings. You keep living the dream. One of the saddest stories in the Bible is Peter on the night Jesus was crucified. Peter heard Jesus say, "It is finished." Do you know where we find Peter next? Back to fishing. He thought, when Jesus said it is finished, he thought Jesus was finished.

CHAPTER FOUR

You got to keep living the dream. People who have no vision for the future always go back to their past. That is what happened to Peter. He had no vision for the future, so he went back to his past even though he once said, "I've left fishing to follow You." Why? He went back because he had no vision for the future.

Then Jesus was resurrected, brought stand up and recovery, and Peter recovered his vision, and he never went back to fishing.

Number three, when you accept responsibility for endings, you begin to think and believe like an overcomer. God wants you to live with the mindset of an overcomer.

I John 5:4 says, "For whatsoever is born of God overcomes the world: and this is the victory that overcomes the world, even our faith."

Romans 8:37 "...in all these things we are more than conquerors through Him who loved us."

It is amazing what happens in us when we quit being passive about our ending and we believe that on the other side of the ending is a new beginning. You come alive! Hope is ignited in your heart. You realize, "I can live again, I can have God's hope and future for my life. This ending is not going to put an end to me. I can, and I will overcome this, no matter how bad it was, no matter how much it hurts, no matter how disappointed I am. It ended, but I did not!"

YOU'VE GOT TO COMMIT TO THE MOUNTAIN

Matthew 13:36, "And Jesus sent the multitude away and went into the house, and His disciples came unto Him saying, declare (or explain) to us the parable of the tares of the field. He answered and said unto them, He that sows the good seed is the Son of Man."

In my life and in your life, through your lifelong relationship with Jesus, He will be sowing good seed into your life. The first form that seed takes is the Word of God. "The sower sows the Word," Jesus said in Mark 4. Jesus the sower, sows the Word of God into your life, and through that Word, He brings you wisdom and understanding and insight. He brings correction and guidance. He brings enlightenment. All of this and much more takes place through the Word of God being sown into our lives.

"And He said unto them, He that sows the good seed is the Son of Man. The field is the world. The good

CHAPTER FIVE

"Sometimes, it is just time to put an end to something."

seed are the children of the kingdom, but the tares are the children of the wicked one. The enemy that sowed them is the devil. The harvest is the end of the world, and the reapers are the angels."

Now, this, of course, is speaking about what I call a macro look at the earth, the end of the ages. But, what is true in the macro is also true in the micro. Not only is this true in the big universal picture of life on earth, it is also true in my life and your life as individuals. Jesus is sowing the good Word of God into our lives, and He sows that Word to bring forth harvest in and through our lives.

When the Word is sown into your life, Jesus begins to reveal Himself to you through and by His Word and by His spirit. As He begins to sow His Word into your life, satan also tries to sow bad seed in your life, right next to Jesus' good seed. Why? Satan does this because he wants to affect the end just like Jesus.

After Rochelle passed away, I began to really think about endings and beginnings. Remember, with every harvest there is an ending, but in that harvest or ending, there is a promise of another beginning. All our lives are full of endings. Eras end. Relationships end. Sometimes they end expectantly, sometimes they end abruptly. Endings sometimes take the form of bankruptcies, divorces, job losses, partnerships dissolve, businesses are no longer viable, the loss of a loved one. Sometimes, it is just time to put an end to something. But the reality is that if we don't understand endings, we end up being afraid of them. A lot of people don't know how to embrace endings or how to react to endings. In the previous chapter, I told you some funny people stories about people not re-acting well to endings. We laugh at those examples, but it is sad to think about the amount of people who come to the end of something, and they don't know what to do. When you come to the end of a something, you are not supposed to stop! You are supposed to keep going. Because we don't know how to handle endings, we are fearful of them.

"Jesus is the beginning and the ending, and He specializes in endings."

Remember, in John 19, on the cross, Jesus said, "It is finished." He didn't say He was finished. Because something ends, because an era ends, that doesn't mean your destiny has ended or that your purpose has ended. Endings can be God-given opportunities to get a new beginning. Many people don't know how to handle endings, so as a result, they end up in chaos. Their life ends in chaos.

Jesus is the beginning and the ending, and He specializes in endings.

CHAPTER FIVE

In the prior chapter, I talked to you about things to know and that will get you through an ending. I want to repeat something to you. Please understand, I am a teacher. As a result, I love to review. I do this because I want your life to stand up and recover or get better! You have to commit to what is on the other side of your ending. You can't keep holding on to the old because if you hold on to the old, you are going to end up living in regret. Endings produce regret like nothing else in life. I also shared with you that you need to take responsibility for endings.

Then we finished in Ecclesiastes 7:8. This is one of the most astounding verses I think I have read. Ecclesiastes 7:8, "The end of a thing can be better than the beginning." What a statement!

Let me say, I never thought that way. I never thought endings could be better than beginnings; but, God says the end of a thing can be better than the beginning. That, in itself, should cause us to look at endings and beginnings in a different light, and as we understand and apply this knowledge to our lives, our lives will go forward.

Let's go back to our original premise – life is full of endings. Most of us have taken care of the big ending. We are ready for that one because we made Jesus the Lord of our lives. We have confidence that He is waiting for us at the end. To be absent from the body is to be present with the Lord; but, that is not the only ending we encounter in life.

Oftentimes, because life is full of endings, it is hard for us to recognize when we need to let go of something. I'm not talking about lying down and quitting because a situation gets difficult. You need to keep that in mind. There is always the pressure on us to quit when we shouldn't quit; but, we also need God's wisdom to discern when something just needs to be let go of. There are some things that just need to be let go of in life.

All of us, me and you and every person who has lived before us and every person who will live after us, we all have eras, or seasons, in our lives that come to an end. Sometimes, it is hard to recognize when it is the Father's will for something to end. We not only have eras and seasons or relationships that come to an end, we have ways of doing things that come to an end.

We need to realize that God may want something to end in our lives so there can be a resurrection of something new and better. I don't want to try to keep something alive that is trying to end. If I do, I won't experience the resurrection that is on the other side of that ending because I'm so busy holding onto something and trying to keep it alive.

I am not talking about quitting because there is pressure or because things get hard. Rather, I don't want to try to keep something alive that is trying to end, because if I do, I won't experience the resurrection that is on the other side of that ending. Anything that God let's die comes with a resurrection on the other side. Let me show you an interesting story that I now see in a different light. I have looked at this differently over the last few years and I hope I can explain it to you. Genesis 22:2, "And God said unto Abraham, take now thy son, thou only son Isaac whom you love, and get you to the land of Moriah and offer him there for a burnt offering upon one of the mountains which I will tell you of."

God asked of Abraham to do something that could only be described as difficult and hard to understand. Let me remind you that Isaac was the son of promise. He was loved by Abraham. He was the hope of the future of Abraham and his family. He had been promised to Abraham, and now God asked Abraham to do this!

"So, Abraham rose up early in the morning, saddled his donkey and took two of the young men with him and Isaac, his son, and clave the wood for the burnt offering and rose up and went unto the place which God had told him. And then, on the third day, Abraham lifted up his eyes and saw the place afar off. And Abraham said unto the young men, stay here with the donkeys and the lad and I will go yonder and worship and will come to you again."

Notice Abraham said, "I and the lad will go and worship and come to you again." So, we see something interesting in the mind of Abraham. Abraham is going to obey God, but he also believes that, on the other side of his obedience, there will be a resurrection of Isaac. Look again at what he said. "I and the lad will go and come to you again."

Verse 9, "And they came to the place which God had told him of. And Abraham built an altar and laid the wood in order. He bound Isaac, his son, laid him on the altar upon the wood. And Abraham stretched forth his hand and took the knife to slay his son."

"And the angel of the Lord called out from heaven and said, Abraham, Abraham. And he said, here am I. He said, lay not your hand upon the lad, neither do thou anything unto him, for now I know..."

"Now I know" is a good thing to hear from God about you.

The complete quote says, "Now I know that you fear God seeing that you have not withheld your son, your only son, from me."

Now, let's look at this in the light of endings and beginnings. Again, Isaac was the son of promise, loved by Abraham, also he was to be instrumental in being a blessing to others. He was the hope of the future, and he had been given to Abraham by God. Abraham was 100 years old when he fathered Isaac. Abraham and Sara having Isaac so late in life had to be a God-thing.

As I looked at this and meditated upon it, I began to wonder what you and I may have in our lives that God began and now may be asking you to lay it down so something better can come in its place.

It is hard sometimes to let go of the thing that has always been your security. It is hard to let go of it. It is easy to believe that because God birthed something, He will always have His hand on it. Yet, what God began may need to go through a new resurrection so that you can have the life He wants you to have.

This challenges a lot of thinking. But, in truth, all of us have had to let things go many times in our lives, even if you weren't thinking about it at the time.

If you are married and have kids, I want to ask you a question. Do you remember pre-kid marriage? Don't worry they can't see what you are reading. Do you remember pre-kid marriage? Perhaps you don't remember that life. Before you had little tax deductions running around the house do you remember having extra money, sleeping in, going on trips, going out to eat and not having to apologize to the waiters for how the room looked when you left. How about no 3:00 a.m. feedings or uninterrupted sex. I am going way back in some of your lives.

We all know people who have had kids and still want to have the pre-kid marriage. They don't want to raise their kids. They don't want to discipline their kids. They don't want to take care of their kids. They want to act like they're still pre-kid married. That's got to end.

Most of us went through that. Do you know why we went through it? The reason is because we were committed to the other side. You were committed to the future. You believed that something better was going to come; and, even though you gave up pre-kid marriage, you were going to get more in this new era, in this new married life, raising those kids together.

As I write these thoughts, I can't help but think about the early days of our church, which we started in 1977. It doesn't seem like 45 years has passed. I don't feel more called now than I did then. In the beginning, I felt like I was supposed to be preaching to thousands, but I wasn't preaching to thousands. I was preaching to dozens, not even hundreds, and I was glad when there were dozens there.

We did church differently back then. We had service and we didn't have praise and worship. We didn't have any musicians. In fact, we didn't have anything. We would start at 7:00 p.m. I would say, "Everybody stand and raise your hands. Let's worship God." No singing, no music. This would last about five minutes, then I would say, "Sit down and open your Bible." I would teach for an hour and a half, and then everyone would go home. I must say that five minutes felt like 30 minutes. It didn't come easy back then, and I was more than willing to give that up. But when God began to bring more people to us, it became hard for me to let go.

Looking back at the more micro level, I recall I had to do some letting go many times over the years. Letting things end or evolve was tough at times. Letting go got more difficult as things became more routine and I grew more comfortable with it. For example, Rochelle and I did not believe in children's church or nursery. We believed the kids ought to be in the service with us. Kids needed to see their parents in church, raising their hands, worshipping God. That is one of those things that sounds good in theory. It's kind of like marriage. We have theoretical views of how marriage should be until you get in it. Then you realize, that's not going to work.

As I recall our succession of endings at our church, I remember having one service on Sunday; and, I really enjoyed it. Then we grew, and the sanctuary couldn't hold any more people. Somebody said to us, "Did you hear about this other church that started having two services on Sunday?" I couldn't wrap my brain around it. Rochelle and I were like, "How do you do that? That's not possible." Yet, all around us were churches that had been having multiple services on Sundays for years, even decades. So, we had to embrace it.

What is my point? Those decisions didn't seem life changing at the time, but at the same time, they were. While it was hard to let go of some of those things, we know now that God had blessed all of it. We had to let things end so there could be a resurrection. And even though God had blessed the marriage Rochelle and I had the first seven years without kids, we had to let that end when kids came, and then He blessed us while we were raising them. Then the kids moved out and we had to let that end. For a lot of parents, they can't ever let go. They have 40-year-old children that they treat as if they were still 14. Why? There is a tendency in us to hold on to something that God has blessed or something that has worked before; but, we've got to let them go.

In my life, I've had to let relationships end. Quite honestly, at one time God blessed those relationships; but, I had to let them end. I had to let go of them so I could have a new beginning and go forward in my life.

Again, I want to make this clear, I am not talking about having a hard season in something and just quitting. I am not talking about that. Because without a doubt, it is a spirit of faithfulness that accomplishes God's purpose in your life. But sometimes we fight to keep something alive that, in fact, has no life in it. It worked once, but it's not working now. Yet we hang on.

I want you to read what I think is one of the most astounding verses that I have read. It is so mentally descriptive to me. It is found in the book of Joel. It is in a part of the Bible people call the minor prophets, which I find hilarious. To me, if you are a prophet and you have a book in the Bible with your name on it, you're not minor. Minor is Charles. Major is Joel.

Joel 1:17, "The seed is rotten under their clods." One translation says, "The seed shrivels under the clods."

A seed that is rotten or a seed that is shriveling is no longer germinating and producing life. Remember, seeds produce harvest.

The book of Haggai 2:19 talks about seed again. "Is the seed yet in the barn? Yes, as yet the vine and the fig tree, the pomegranate and the olive tree have not borne fruit?"

CHAPTER FIVE

This time, He says the problem is that the seed is still in the barn and, as a result, there is no fruit.

Let's talk about those two truths. When I think about the seed shriveling under the clods, I want to ask you a couple of questions. Do you have seeds that are shriveling in the clods in your life? By that I mean, are there areas in your life where you are going through the motions? The words are there, the activity is there, and yet, in fact, there is no life. It may have worked before, but it's not working now. The seed is shriveling under the clods. It's not producing the harvest that it has produced before or that you think it should be producing now.

Why are those seeds not producing? Why are they not bearing fruit? It is because you need to let it go. You still have new blessed seed in the barn that you now need to sow into your life! When something ends, especially something we didn't want to end, we tend to hold on to it. I went through that. I didn't want to let Rochelle go, even though she was in heaven. I was still holding on to what was and thinking about what could have been. I also struggled with guilt because I was here, enjoying our grandkids, our family, our church, our friends. I grieved for her because she was missing all these wonderful moments we planned for in our lives.

I was tormented with this for two years. As we drew near to the second anniversary of her death, I came home from our Christmas Eve services, that were overflowing in attendance, and I sat down in my bedroom and I began to weep like I had never wept before. Somehow, I ended up on the floor and I cried from depths I did not know I had. I don't know how long I was there. Suddenly, I was aware that Jesus was in my room. I don't know how to describe this to you, other than, His presence was so real and tangible, I looked up, expecting to see Him. He was not there physically, but He was definitely in my bedroom.

He then said to me, very gently, "Charles, have you forgotten, Rochelle is happy, no, she is very happy! Charles, we want you happy, no, we want you to be very happy! In fact, we need you to be happy. Charles, be happy!" There, I felt Him walk out of my bedroom. In a moment, I sat up and I said, "Enough is enough. I have wept enough, I have grieved enough." That night, I let go of what was gone. I still love her, and I enjoy memories, but I let go. I have new seed that needs to get out of the barn, to replace the seed that is no longer producing and has shriveled in the ground.

Across the church and secular world, there are truths we can learn from for our lives and families. Let me talk to you from my church world. In the church world, there have been churches and movements that God blessed and God used and they produced great fruit. Now, when we look at them, we see they need to be propped up, meaning, they are merely going through the motions. They have all kinds of activity, but there is no life. I am not saying this judgmentally.

We see this also in the business world. People had a business, and they did it a certain way, and it was good, and it produced. But now, they are going through the motions, meaning, there is activity, but there's no life. What is missing? They didn't get the new seed out of the barn. They have seed, but it's shriveling under the clods. The seed is not germinating or producing.

Let's bring it down to our lives. I am going to be blunt with you. I've seen this happen and so have you. I've watched people that did marriage a certain way and now they're going through the motions. All the words are there, all the motion is there, but there's no life. They keep trying, they keep holding on to something that they need to let go of. Not let go of the marriage, but let go of the way they are doing their marriage. That way needs to end so God can bring a resurrection to a better life that He has for them now.

Does that make sense to you now? Years ago, when we were in our first building and we needed to add another service, that seemed like the biggest thing in the world to us, but we had to do it. I could have dug my heels in and said no. I could have said I like having everybody together and this is what we're going to keep doing. "If God wants us to grow, He needs to give us a bigger building."

We would have never obtained a bigger building. How could we get a bigger building? We couldn't get a bigger building because we didn't have the amount of people coming so we could get a bigger building. Do you see what I'm saying? If I had held on to what needed to die, our seeds would have withered in the ground.

You can get stuck on something, because it worked once or it works for ten years, but it is not working now. Again, I'm not talking about quitting because you're in a hard season. I'm talking about being smart enough with God's wisdom and God's discernment in your life to realize that this seed is shriveling in the clod, and you need to get the new seed out of the barn and get it in the ground because the old seed is not working anymore. You need to get the new seed in the ground.

Can I take you deeper? When I was first looking at these truths, I asked, "How and why do things die? How and why do things end?" I offer to you what I discovered.

Number 1, Natural life cycle. Grass withers. Flowers fade. Things end because of the natural life cycle in the earth.

Number 2, By attack. An invasion, war, persecution, conflicts, can also bring endings.

Number 3, Sometimes, things end because of the judgment of God.

Number 4, Things end because the Father has pronounced that it needs to end, so resurrection can happen.

The reality is, that there are times in our lives, when we need to let something go. We shouldn't let things die because of neglect or because of discouragement or because it seemed like a good idea at the time. We need His wisdom. I think that wisdom begins by asking myself, honestly, "Is the seed shriveling in the clods?" I have activity. I'm very busy, but there's no life.

Heavy thoughts, aren't they?

When I started looking at these truths, it was in the context of wanting to get more fruit out of my life. I didn't want seed shriveling in the clods. I do not want to get to that point in my life. Why get to that point? The Bible says it can happen, but why go there? Why not do a preemptive strike? Why not get ahead of this? Why come to that place in your marriage, your health, your kids? Why not do a preemptive strike and start watching and planning before you get to that place? Why wait until you are forced to do something or you miss it? Why not get ahead of it?

I want to share with you a part of my journey down this path. When I began seeing these truths, I began to see I needed to make some changes in our church leadership. Don't get me wrong. I was not ready to give up my leadership position in our church. In fact, at that time, I was doing better than I had done for years, and I am still full of life and God is still using me. Yet, as I began to think about these truths, I began to realize the Lord, for several weeks, had been speaking to me about different ways of leading our church. I believe it was because I had prayed, "God, don't let me shrivel in the clods. I don't want to change because I have to. I want to change because I need to." Also, remember my original prayer, "Father, I can't screw this up. Help me." He was/is still responding to that prayer!

As I began seeking the Lord about all this, He began to speak to me about different ways of leading. I will be very frank with you, for that to happen, I had to be willing to let go of some areas that had always been my territory. My natural reaction was, "Don't get close to this. That's mine. That's my holy ground." I was not fighting our worship pastor over praise and worship. If I could sing, I probably would have, but I'm not fighting him over that. I wasn't fighting our nursery and childcare pastor over those areas. I was more than willing to let them take care of the babies and the little kids.

You were not going to find me out in the bookstore or coffee shops. I wasn't going to take over usher or guest services or follow-up. Our Spanish Ministry Pastor didn't have to worry about me moving in; but, there were areas that were mine, particularly the preaching and teaching and the daily vision casting.

As I was looking at my life, I had to ask myself if I was willing to let go of some areas that had always been mine so that new life and new seeds that were in the barn can be planted, before the seeds that were already growing and bearing fruit started to shrivel. I don't want to get to the "shriveling stage" and then start looking for the new seed in the barn. I would rather get new seed in the ground before the old seed shrivels.

CHAPTER FIVE

Let me tell you it's not easy to let go of something you have always done, and I will tell you, it's harder than it sounds. That is why we try to hold onto things we need to let go of. You've got to commit to the God of the new beginning. Let something better come to pass.

In Acts 2, Peter quotes David who quoted a Messianic psalm. It was a prophesy concerning the life of Jesus when He would come.

Acts 2:25, "For David speaketh concerning Him. I foresaw the Lord always before my face. He is on my right hand that I should not be moved. Therefore, did my heart rejoice, my tongue was glad. Moreover, also my flesh shall rest in hope because You will not leave my soul in hell, neither will You suffer thine holy one to see corruption."

He is talking about how Jesus would look at the end of His life.

Verse 28, "You have made known to me the ways of life. You shall make me full of joy with thy countenance."

In these verses, we discover seven things that Jesus did, that we need to do when we come to endings in our lives.

Number one, keep looking at the Father. Endings will try to get you to look at the ending. No. Keep looking at the Father. Don't get distracted by the ending. Keep looking at your Father.

Number two, expect for His strength to take you through the ending into the new beginning.

Number three, worship. Spend extra time in worship. Do you know why? Because the more time you spend in worship, the less time you will spend worrying and being full of anxiety about the ending.

Number four, hope. Have a positive expectation of what is on the other side of the ending. "I'm going to let go of the way I have been doing marriage, and I'm going to find a new way to do it. We are going to find a new way. This way worked once. It is not working now. We are going to get new seed in our soil, and God is going to take us through. We are going to keep our eyes on the Father. I am going to find a new way to do business. I am going to find a new way to live healthy. I am going to find a new way to plan my financial future. What has worked, isn't working now. I have to get new seed in the ground, and it's going to bear fruit."

Number five, commit to the resurrection. There is a new beginning for me on the other side of this ending. I am committed to that resurrection!

Number six, expect God's direction. He will guide you. He will lead you.

Number seven, on the other side of your ending, believe you will be satisfied. Look at Jesus. He said, "You have made known to me the ways of life. You will make me full of joy with your presence. I will have satisfaction."

CHAPTER FIVE

This is my prayer for you as you continue reading this book, "Father, in the Name of Jesus, we commit. We commit to the other side of our ending. We embrace endings. We are not afraid of them. We commit to the resurrection on the other side. You are the beginning and the ending. Speak to me in my heart. Show us if there are seeds in our lives that are shriveling that we need to replace with new seeds, so that we can get a new harvest. Don't let us waste our lives holding onto things that once worked that aren't working anymore. In Jesus' Name, Amen."

As I began to open my heart, the Lord led me to let go of some areas of our church that had been exclusively mine. It wasn't as hard as I thought it would be because I knew it needed to happen. I wasn't going to wait until the seed shriveled. No.

I installed my children, Shannon and Jared, as the lead pastors of our church, which has resulted in new seeds being sown, more fruit being produced than ever before in our churches. I keep on sharing the teaching and preaching duties with them, which has resulted in their gifts being revealed to our church family and to the world. The list of new fruit and more fruit is too much for me to cover in this book.

Can this happen for you? Of course! Please believe with me, that no matter how painful your ending was, there is a new beginning waiting for you. Embrace it! Declare right now – "Enough is enough. I let go of what was and I reach forth for what is before me, my new beginning, created for me by Jesus, my ending, and my beginning. I am ready for the new seed that Jesus is going to sow into my heart. I am not going to live any longer grieving over the past. I choose a new beginning."

As I have previously stated, every one of us knows life is full of endings, endings of eras, endings of relationships. Sometimes those endings are expected. Sometimes they are abrupt, and we did not expect them. This book is helping us look at this in the light of Jesus being our stand up and recovery when we have endured an ending and are ready for our new beginning. Do you see how these two truths regarding Jesus work together? Recovery could also be called a new beginning! Jesus never intended for an ending to "end" us.

Endings, as we know, can come in the form of the loss of a loved one, bankruptcies, divorce, job loss, partnerships dissolving, businesses that did well for a while and are no longer viable. The list goes on and on. Sometimes it is just time to put an end to something. But we generally, tend to be fearful of endings. Remember in John 19, Jesus said, "It is finished." He, Himself, was not finished! "It" in your life can end, but that doesn't mean your destiny has ended. The end of an era or relationship is not the end of a destiny, not the end of a purpose, not the end of your life.

Endings can be God-given opportunities for a new beginning. People don't know how to handle endings, as a result, they end up in chaos. When you get to an ending in your life, you are not supposed to stop!

I like to review with you, it keeps the thought alive in you and you may be reading this book a few pages at a time, so it's good to review. Plus, repetition is a proven way to learn. Remember how you learned your multiplications? Repetition.

To get through an ending, and experience your new beginning, you have to be committed to what is on the other side of that ending. You can't hold onto the old because that will produce regret. That is quite a thought.

Ecclesiastes 7:8 says, "The end of a thing can be better than the beginning."

We need to remember that God may want something to end so there can be a resurrection. I don't want to try to keep something alive that is trying to end. If I do, I won't experience the resurrection that comes after the ending.

Again, I'm not talking about quitting just because you are going through a hard period. Don't struggle to keep something alive that has no life in it. The end is hard to accept sometimes.

In the last chapter, we saw Joel 1:17, "The seed shrivels under the clods." Also Haggai 2:17 says, "The seed is in the barn." Here we see two different emphases on seed.

It is possible to have seed shriveling in the clods. What a mental image those words paint. What is this in life? We are going through the motions. The words are there. The activity is there. But there's no life. Why? There are things that need to be let go of. We need to ask, "What is missing?" What is missing is the new blessed seed that is still in the barn, but we are still trying to get life out of the old seed that has shriveled in the clods.

I'm sure that, you, like me, would agree that not all endings are pleasant. I have seen movies that made me happy when finally ended. I have been in a few church services I couldn't wait to end. But not all endings are pleasant. They can bring what seems to be or is, a darkness or dark days, even chaos, to our lives. There is a big difference between the end of a season, no matter how dark it looks, and the completion of a destiny or the finished work of Christ in your life.

Let me say that again. There is a big difference between the end of a season or an era in your life, no matter how dark it looks, and the completion of your destiny or the work of Christ in your life.

Often, myself included, we respond badly to endings because of three things:

Number one, bad information. I've had people say things to me that are astonishingly bad! I don't say that judgmentally. It is what people say about an ending that saddens me, like, "God has abandoned me. God has left me."

That is a bad response to an ending, and they have a bad response because of bad teaching. They have been taught the reason why the ending occurred was because God abandoned them. God walked away from them.

Listen, don't go with opinion. Go with scripture. Jesus said, "When I come into your life, I will never leave you. I will never forsake you."

We respond badly to endings because of number two, wrong focus. By wrong focus, I mean we start looking for someone or something to blame for an ending. Instead of focusing on our new beginning, we are focusing on someone to blame. Remember David's men at Ziklag? They blamed David when they should have blamed the Amalekites.

Number three, people respond badly to endings because they have the wrong assessment of themselves. They think that because an ending has come into their life, they are diminished in value or they are, by nature now a failure. If you don't know this, you need to. For the sake of teaching, do we agree no one lives a life of 100 percent success every day, all day? No one does. I don't care how strong in faith you are. None of us are stronger in faith than the Apostle Paul, and he had some bad days as we have already looked at. No one has nothing but success.

Why do people think that because they've had an ending, that somehow, now they're a failure? No. You had an ending which puts you in line for a stand up and recovery and a new beginning.

Why am I focusing on people responding badly? Because when you respond badly, either through bad information or wrong focus or the wrong assessment of ourselves, you will bring bitterness into your life. Bitterness is always a wrong response to an apparent negative.

All of these things — bad information, wrong focus, wrong assessment of ourselves — ignore an incredible Bible truth. We should not be afraid of endings. I will show you why.

Hebrews 10:9, "Then said he, Lo, I come to do thy will, O, God. He takes away the first that He may establish the second." In this verse, He is talking primarily about taking away the law so that He may establish the New Covenant. It is a principle we see throughout scripture.

Let us be clear, not everything that is taken out of our life was by God. There is a devil in the earth that comes to steal, to kill and to destroy (John 10:10). Sometimes God will remove something because He wants to establish something greater or better.

Many people try to hold onto the first. There are people today who would bring back the law of Moses if

CHAPTER SIX

they could have their way. They would. I'm not exaggerating. One night at a UTEP basketball game, I was verbally assaulted by four kids who seemed to be college age. They had come to our church when I was teaching a verse-by-verse study on the book of Hebrews. I had taught from the Book of Hebrews and talked about how we were no longer under the law of animal sacrifice. When they saw me at the game, they sat down behind me at halftime and verbally attacked me, saying I was a heretic, that I was misleading people, and that God wanted animal sacrifice and the law was still active.

I was trying to be sweet, considering my wife and my little kids were there with me. What I really wanted to do was knock the fire out of each of them. I am at a basketball game. Leave me alone. I didn't find them and go over to harass them at a basketball game. Leave me alone.

Finally, there was another pastor from another church here in El Paso who was sitting one row back. He stood up along with his associate pastor, sat down between me and them, and said to them, "You, four, up. Out. These are not your seats. Get out or I'm getting an usher." So, they got up and left.

"Thank you," I said.

They said, "That was horrible."

As they were leaving, one of them said, "I can't wait until we get to heaven and then we get to offer animal sacrifices again."

I replied, "If all of that was so great, why did Jesus say it is finished?" She stood there speechless.

There are always people who want to hold onto the first. If you hold onto what God has taken, then you are never going to get the second, which is better, which is greater.

Now, I want to show you something really amazing in the Book of Genesis.

Genesis 1:5, "And God called the light day and the darkness He called night, and the evening and the morning were the first day."

So, He called light, day, and He called darkness, night.

Verse 8, "And God called the firmament heaven, and the evening and the morning were the second day."

Verse 13, "And the evening and the morning were the third day."

Verse 23, "And the evening and the morning were the fifth day."

Look at verse 31, "And God saw everything He had made, and behold, it was very good. And the evening and the morning were the sixth day."

Do you notice a pattern in these verses? The pattern that jumps out at us is this: We look at days as mornings and evenings. God looks at days as evenings and mornings. Now, this is significant for our understanding because we believe that day starts in the light and ends in the darkness. God says that out of darkness will come light. We see our lives progressing from light to darkness.

Consider, our lives progress from darkness toward light.

God looks at life, surprise, surprise, totally different than we do. That's a shocker! God looks at our lives from a whole different perspective.

We tend to not like darkness. I am not saying God loves darkness. I am saying God is not afraid of darkness, because God knows, on the other side of darkness, you are coming into light. We see light ending, "Oh, my God, it's dark." Something ends and we're afraid. God says, when there is an end, that's okay because light is coming. Your life will not end in darkness. Your day, your life, is not going to end in darkness. It is going to end in light.

Our lives are moving from darkness to light. In the Hebrew text, the word "darkness" also means "chaos" and the word "light" comes from the Hebrew word that means "order." God is saying that when you are in chaos, by God being in your ending, you are going to move toward order. You are going to move toward better. Things are going to get better. You are moving toward light. The day is not over because you are at an ending.

It is not over because Jesus is the beginning and ending, ending and beginning in the same instant.

"Oftentimes, darkness or chaos in our lives is not the end of something, but, in fact, is the start of something."

You may be reading this book and you would declare your life is in darkness. There may be even a form of chaos in your life. Do not be afraid of it. See Jesus in it with you! He didn't bring it, but He surely has a new beginning, a stand up, a recovery for you.

Sometimes when things end, we don't know what to do with ourselves. I felt that way when Rochelle went to heaven. There are endings that God brings and, of course, there are endings that the devil brings. But no matter who brings it, Jesus is Lord of each one, and He can still bring light, even out of the darkness the devil brought.

God's day starts with darkness. Oftentimes, darkness or chaos in our lives is not the end of something, but, in fact, is the start of something. The darkness you are in can be what is going to usher in your new beginning.

Here is what we know about creation. If you never thought of it, think about it now. Everything in Genesis 1 that God did, all of creation, was done in progression. Each act of creation was built on the previous act, and all of it was moving toward verse 31, where it all became "very good."

So, in my life, God moved me from a darkness into a light, a darkness to a light, a darkness to a light. Each one is a day, and it is all moving toward that which is "very good," and each day builds upon the previous day.

If we can see Him in our endings, we can see what He can do even in dark times. That day of darkness in your life or the darkness in your life right now could, in fact, become the beginning of your new day.

Psalm 16:7, "I will bless the Lord Who has given me counsel. My reins (heart) also instructs me in the night seasons (or, when it is dark)." In the night seasons, our hearts can instruct us.

Nighttime, dark, that is when we have to be established in our hearts because in the dark, in the night, that is when we get confused. Not only literal dark or night. We can be "in the dark" when the sun is shining. Darkness can be mental, emotional. I remember feeling like I was in the dark after losing Rochelle. I was going through life, at times, not even aware of my surroundings. Why? I was caught up in the loss, the guilt, the regret, the fear of my future, or even if I had a future. Looking back, I realize, satan was sitting in my ending. All of these emotions I just listed, none of them are of God. I did what I am encouraging you to do. I remembered Jesus gives me stand up, recovery, a new day. He is moving to the completion of my "day." I made myself quit accepting darkness as the end of my "day" and chose light, just like David chose to be recovered where everyone else chose to be bitter. If I could do it, and David could do it, you can do it!

Luke 5:36, "He spoke a parable unto them saying, no man puts a piece of new garment upon an old. If, otherwise, then both the new makes a tear, and the piece that was taken out of the new agrees not with the old. And no man puts new wine into old bottles (or old wineskins). Else, the new wine will burst the bottles and be spilled, and the bottles shall be perished (or shall be ruined). But new wine must be put into new bottles (or new wineskins) and both are preserved."

Verse 39, "No man, having drunk old wine, straightway desires the new. For he says, the old is better."

The old is better. I want it the way I want it to be. The old is better.

I want life the way it used to be! I know, but we aren't going back!

"Give me that old-time religion." No, I don't want old-time religion. Old-time religion was little buildings, a hundred people, hardwood pews, boring preachers who were mad at everybody. Girls couldn't cut their hair, couldn't wear makeup, weren't allowed to lead. People were under the law, trying to earn God's love and blessings. I like new better.

CHAPTER SIX

But there are people who want the old because that's what they tasted. That is what they knew. That is what life was. Therefore, when things end, we're uncomfortable with it until we see Jesus is in that ending. Maybe He didn't bring the ending to pass, but that doesn't mean that because He didn't bring the ending, that He can't sit in the ending, or He won't be Lord of the ending. Absolutely. He can and will.

The new wine He wants to bring into your life won't fit in your old wineskins.

You may be reading this book and you have been thinking that your church just doesn't seem to do for you what it used to do for you. What's wrong with the church? There is nothing wrong with the church. God is trying to take you out of that old wineskin. You don't want to give up the old wine and the old wineskin because that is what you remember. That is what you knew. That is what you drank. But He has a new wine He wants to put in a new wineskin. Why are you trying to hold on that old level of relationship with Him when He is calling you to a higher level, a greater level, a better level? He has taken your satisfaction away from you with the old wine because He wants to give you new wine. You have to become open and welcome a new wineskin. He can't put new wine in you because you can't handle it. We can't see this because we are comfortable with the old, the familiar and we like it better.

What happens when you try to take the old wine and put it in the old wineskin? The old wineskin splits, and is destroyed, and the wine is spilled and wasted.

We see this all around us. We've all seen businesses that didn't take the new wine into new wineskins and they're dying, or they are already gone.

Do you find yourself saying, "You know, this always worked with my wife. Now it doesn't seem to affect her." Maybe she is ready for some new wine and new wineskins. Whether you realize it or not, she is a new wineskin now, and you have got to find that new wine.

I say to you, if I did anything right in the 42 years I was married to Rochelle, I did that well. I never got hung up on old wineskins and old wine. If that girl was moving, growing, changing, I was moving with her.

We see this all the time, right? The way people do things, the way they practice things, in truth, they are trying to put new wine in their old wineskins and the new is going to be spilled.

I've had many great years pastoring in our church. As I look back over the 45 years, it's like all the good things run together. They stack one upon another, so many good things. I always stop and make my staff stop, and we breathe, and we take time to be grateful to God. We never take good for granted. Even though He is good and does good (Psalm 119:68), I think it's wrong to take good for granted.

I also I have to tell you, I've had to pastor our church through some dark days. Dark days, when it was hard to see, and it was difficult to understand what was going on. When you are in darkness, that is

CHAPTER SIX

when you need to remember and know that light is coming, and that God starts the day with darkness and ends it with light.

"No matter how hard winter tries to hold on, spring always comes."

For years, I looked at life as light to dark. Do you know what that does? It discourages you. In fact, after darkness is light. You need to see Jesus in the ending and know that morning is coming.

Looking back, I can see the new. It is easy to see it when looking back; but, when you're in the darkness, that is when you have to walk by faith and trust that God's day has just begun. Oh, my God, what a thought!

God works in cycles. Spring always comes. No matter how hard winter tries to hold on, spring always comes. Light, a new beginning, is on its way. It's not that far away!

God works in cycles. Winter to spring, spring to summer, summer to fall, fall to winter, winter to spring, as long as the earth remains. Night to day, day to night. The laws of seed time and harvest (Genesis 8:22).

If you don't understand how this works or if you forget, then bitterness will come to stay and will sit in your ending, or you will begin to blame somebody and you will have the wrong ending in your life.

Throughout creation, there was a darkness that brought forth the day. Every day is progressive. This day that you're living right now is built on days you have already lived. But this day is going to be used for the days coming in front of you. They are all progressive.

God builds. That is the reason your end is supposed to be better than your beginning. Here are some more verses for you:

Matthew 5:6, "Jesus said, when you are hungry and thirsty, you shall be filled." The fact is spiritual fullness comes out of hunger and thirsting. If you are not hungry and thirsty, God won't fill you. If you are hungry and thirsty, you will get filled.

II Corinthians 12:10, Paul said, "When I am weak, then I am strong." Even though Paul was in a place of weakness or darkness, he went to strength and light.

Psalm 30:5, "Though you weep in the night, joy will come in the morning."

I realize that people reading this book will be on opposite ends of the life spectrum. There will be people reading this book and their lives are the best they have been. There will be others who are in a real dark place in their lives.

If you are in darkness, light is coming! I can say that not as a cute saying, but I say that based on Genesis 1. If you are in darkness, light is coming! Your day has not ended. In fact, God has declared it is just beginning. Your day is beginning.

If your life is good right now, keep looking for the new wine and the new wineskins. Don't think that what you have will stay the same forever. It doesn't. God takes us from glory to glory, from faith to faith. If something is taken, even if by the devil, your Jesus can bring a new beginning. If an evening comes, He will bring a morning.

We need to be careful. We tend **to like** the old better. What it takes is a change of **our perspe**ctive, so we are to be excited about the new **and** not trying to hold onto the old.

Never underestimate what God can do out of a loss. Again, never underestimate what God can do for you out of a loss!

My prayer for you:

> My Heavenly Father, I know, as people are reading this book, that they are living their lives on every level of life. I pray for each person, that no matter where they are in life, I pray all of them will remember these truths, and that none of us will

ever look at days the same way again. I believe we will never be afraid of endings again. We will not be afraid of them because You are always in the ending as You are always in the beginning.

I pray we will have this confidence, that even though the first may be gone, that You Father will establish the second. You will establish the second. You will bring it to pass.

Lord, I pray for those who they feel they are in a place of darkness right now. I'm excited to be able to say to them — Don't be afraid. Light is on its way to you. Light is coming. Darkness cannot stop it. Darkness cannot stop your light from coming.

Help us, Lord, as we go through life to not be afraid because You are our ending and our beginning.

I know, Lord, that there are some relationships that are, in fact, going through transition from old wine to new wine in their lives. Give them the strength and the wisdom to see it and embrace it and take it where You want it to be.

We are not going to try to hold onto the old. We are going to embrace the new. The light is coming. The stand up is coming. Recovery is coming. The new day is coming. The new beginning is coming.

In Jesus' Name. Amen.

I pray you are receiving the light of God's hope and promise of a new beginning in your life.

Jesus is your Stand-Up and Recovery. He is the life that satisfies, dwelling in your life. Jesus is in your Endings, ready to give you a New Beginning!

As you can imagine there were many people that came along beside and helped me to get from my place of hurt, depression, and trauma. I want to thank my amazing children who, while receiving their own healing, were critical to my restoration. My daughter, Shannon, my son, Jared, his wife Karla, and their children, Caleb, Emery, Grayson and Charlotte; I cannot express how much I love you all and how blessed I am to have you as children and grandchildren. Rochelle is so proud of all of you!

Also, a special thanks and a debt of gratitude to my Pastor Tommy Barnett, Pastor Don Caywood, and Pastor Dave Whaley who called me everyday and listened to me when I cried and always offered me encouragement, while speaking hope into my future.

Dr. Mitch Farrell, your counsel, which combined with medical science and scriptures was invaluable. Thank you!

I also want to thank the people of Abundant Church. You have loved me, supported me and believed in me for over 45 years. We walked this path to recovery and restoration together.

About the Author

Charles Nieman is an author, motivational speaker, community leader and the founder of Abundant Church, a non-denominational community.

Over 40 years ago he committed his life to the study of the Bible and pursuit of knowing God more intimately. Those commitments are how he has managed to press through some of life's darkest and most trying times, in turn gaining the wisdom needed to guide people, both through his words and by example, to the abundant life God desires for humanity.

He is the visionary for Abundant Worship, The Abundant Conference, and the expansion of Abundant Church to now, four campuses throughout West and Central Texas. He has traveled the world speaking to thousands on 6 out of 7 continents on the planet.

Nieman leads the Abundant Church family along with his son and daughter, Jared and Shannon Nieman.